W9-BVQ-809

MANAGEMENT REDISCOVERED

HOW COMPANIES CAN ESCAPE THE NUMBERS TRAP

MANAGEMENT REDISCOVERED
HOW COMPANIES CAN ESCAPE THE NUMBERS TRAP

Donald A. Curtis

Dow-Jones Irwin
Homewood, Illinois 60430

Dow Jones-Irwin is a trademark of Dow Jones & Company, Inc.

This publication is designed to provide accurate and
authoritative information in regard to the subject matter
covered. It is sold with the understanding that the
publisher is not engaged in rendering legal, accounting, or
other professional service. If legal advice or other expert
assistance is required, the services of a competent
professional person should be sought.

*From a Declaration of Principles jointly adopted by a Committee
of the American Bar Association and a Committee of Publishers.*

Sponsoring editor: Jim Childs
Project editor: Joan Hopkins
Production manager: Diane Palmer
Jacket design: Sam Concialdi
Compositor: Carlisle Communications, Ltd.
Typeface: 11/13 Century Schoolbook
Printer: R. R. Donnelley & Sons Company

Library of Congress Cataloging-in-Publication Data

Curtis, Donald A.
    Management rediscovered : how companies can escape the numbers
trap / Donald A. Curtis.
        p.   cm.
    ISBN 1-55623-276-4
    1. Industrial management—United States.   I. Title.
HD70.U5C87   1990
658.4'00973—dc20   89-37611
                                                                CIP

Printed in the United States of America
1 2 3 4 5 6 7 8 9 0 DO 6 5 4 3 2 1 0 9

This Book Is Dedicated to My Wife Joan—My Best Friend.

ACKNOWLEDGMENTS

This book is the product of a lifetime of experience in the American business community. During this time I have been influenced by an enormous number of people, many of whom have passed on. It would be impossible to acknowledge them all. However, I would like to mention a few:

Malcom Stamper, president of the Boeing Company (retired); William Luneburg, president and CEO of American Motors (deceased); Daniel Rowe, president of Sterns; my partners Daniel Gruber, who reviewed the manuscript in detail, Charles L. Biggs, Pat A. Loconto, John C. Shaw, and Thomas Sleight; my colleagues Steven Gottlieb, Michael De Cavalcante, and Michael Esposito; and my secretary Mamie Manchion.

This book was written primarily at the Murray Hill Inn in New Providence, New Jersey, where the management and staff not only adopted me and my project in a very heartwarming way, but also were incredibly helpful as I tried to write and continue my management consulting activities. A very special thanks goes to Kenny Lee, general manager, and his staff—especially Eileen Shea, Barbara Byleckie, Joyce Stambaugh, Linda Kress, Laura Donatelli, Julie Marango, Cindy Arches, Steven Trush, Denise Martin, Douglas Bigham, Eva Frances, Michael Hanna, and Teresa Perry.

PREFACE

Through most of the 1980s it has been popular to criticize the management of American companies. American managers have been accused of everything from being too interested in their short-run financial results to being ignorant of the technical details of their businesses. However, we are using the same management system that, until ten years ago, was the envy of the developed world and had been for decades. Foreigners, including the Japanese, had clamored to visit our companies and attend our schools of business administration. What happened?

I believe that there is an undiagnosed disease in the American management system, and like an athlete with an undiagnosed diabetic condition, we will never reach our competitive potential until we understand and treat it. For years I have been concerned that our system was not as good as everyone, including ourselves, believed. Some of the central themes of the book can be traced to talks about American management that I gave in the middle and late 1970s. Indeed, in 1980 when Robert Hayes and Robert Abernathy published their landmark article, "Managing Our Way To Economic Decline," my son Mark called me and said: "Dad, some guys just wrote an article about what you have been saying."

As the flood of business advice books, such as the much acclaimed *In Search of Excellence,* appeared in the early 1980s, I thought that we were finally coming to grips with the fact that our management system needed reevaluation and rebuilding. As the 1980s progressed, however, I grew convinced that this was not really happening. What we were doing instead was focusing on the undesirable results that our management process seemed to produce and then telling each other that we needed new management techniques to do better.

This approach will not materially improve our management process any more than an aspirin will improve a cold. The question is *why* we are having these outcomes in the first place? Why is it even necessary to discuss things like:

- Overfocus on short-run earnings
- Neglect of product portfolios
- Loss of domestic markets to foreign competitors

when we all know these outcomes are bad without being told?

What we should be discussing are the characteristics of the American management process which routinely produces these undesirable results. It is very difficult to do something constructive about a problem unless one has a good idea of what is causing it. In this case, we seem to be trying to change outcomes without being willing or able to come to grips with what is *causing* our "American management problem" in the first place. Hence, this book was written. *I believe I know what is causing our problem, and Part I of this book is my description of what I think it is.*

While this book is intended for people who are reasonably knowledgeable about the American management process, this book is not difficult to read. The real difficulty will be in reacting to the cause of our problem because it is at the very heart of our management system. Part II of the book is intended to be helpful in this regard.

Throughout the text I use the pronoun "we" to mean all members of the American business community, including: managers, lenders, investors, and members of the business management intellectual community, such as business writers and business school professors. This obviously includes me, because as a practicing management consultant since 1957, I have certainly been part of the generation who got us where we are today.

Donald A. Curtis
November 1989

CONTENTS

PART I
THE ANALOGUE PROBLEM   1

CHAPTER 1   THE ANALOGUE MANAGEMENT TRAP   3
CHAPTER 2   THE AMERICAN ACCOUNTING SYSTEM—A
             BADLY FLAWED ANALOGUE   20
CHAPTER 3   THE EFFECT OF ANALOGUE MANAGEMENT ON
             AMERICAN CORPORATIONS   33
CHAPTER 4   THE MYTH OF "GROWTH" AS A MEASURE OF
             CORPORATE SUCCESS   50
CHAPTER 5   THE COMMONLY USED ANALOGUES ARE
             TECHNICALLY FLAWED   61

PART II
ESCAPING THE ANALOGUE TRAP   79

CHAPTER 6   USING ANALOGUES IN A MORE INSIGHTFUL
             FASHION   85
CHAPTER 7   GETTING THE MANAGEMENT REPORTS RIGHT   95
CHAPTER 8   MANAGING THE LARGEST SINGLE COST—
             OVERHEAD   119
CHAPTER 9   SEIZING THE OPPORTUNITY TO BETTER
             MANAGE SERVICE   137
CHAPTER 10   CONTINUOUS COMPETITIVE ADVANTAGE   149
CHAPTER 11   CORE COMPETITIVE POLICIES AND
             HORIZONTAL MANAGEMENT   167
CHAPTER 12   THOUGHTS ON IMPLEMENTATION   184

             INDEX   195

PART I

THE ANALOGUE PROBLEM

CHAPTER 1

THE ANALOGUE
MANAGEMENT TRAP

The American business management process is based on two false premises. Our failure to identify and question these premises is the underlying reason why American companies have difficulty competing successfully in the world market.

For 30 years after World War II, it was impossible to evaluate American management. American companies faced no real foreign competition in their home markets and in the rest of the world.[1] However, there were many reasons to support the belief that the American management process was superior and little evidence existed to indicate otherwise. The United States had played a crucial role in World War II and its industrial might seem to be the major reason behind this leadership position. Further, Americans had always shown much more interest in the business management process than other developed countries as evidenced by the thriving business press and the popularity of business administration as a university major.[2]

---

[1] It is worth noting that essentially everyone concerned with the business management process today—managers themselves, business journalists and academics, even investors—came to maturity during or since this period.

[2] Since 1954, business administration has been the most popular university major and since 1964 the Masters Degree in Business Administration (MBA) has been the most popular graduate degree.

However, as our foreign competitors recovered from World War II and began to compete in the United States and around the world, it became clear that something was wrong. Americans were losing in market after market. Between 1970 and 1979 the share of the domestic automobile market held by American manufacturers went from 85 percent to 78 percent; their share of the domestic consumer electronics market from 73 percent to 49 percent. Meanwhile, the U.S. share of world exports of manufactured product went from 21.3 percent in 1970 to 17.3 percent in 1979. Even more worrisome was the failure of America's productivity, and consequently its standard of living, to continue to grow as the 1970s wore on. In the 1960s productivity increases per person-hour averaged 3.2 percent per year. In the 1970s it was .9 percent.

After a period of confusion about identifying the fundamental problem, people began to focus on the American management process.[3] American managers were accused of:

- Being too short-run oriented.
- Not being interested in their employees.
- Being reluctant to replace obsolete but still operational equipment.
- Being neglectful of their product portfolios.
- Not being responsive to the changing needs and desires of their customers.
- Being too interested in manipulating their corporate structure.
- Being ignorant of the technical realities of their businesses.

American managers responded to the criticism in many ways. There were trips to Japan to better understand what the Japanese were really doing. Business advice books were suddenly best sellers for the first time in history. Managers

---

[3]The landmark article in this regard appeared in the July–August 1980 issue of the *Harvard Business Review* "Managing Our Way to Economic Decline" by Robert H. Hayes and William J. Abernathy.

took action. Corporate staffs were slashed ruthlessly, as were middle management jobs, the prevalence of which is a hallmark of our management process. Unproductive plants were closed. Many companies were restructured by management to focus on their mainline business and to free undermanaged (and therefore undervalued) assets presumably for more productive uses. Companies talked of adopting quality programs and using "Just In Time" material management techniques. Some American companies returned production to the United States which had previously been "out sourced" to foreign plants.

The average quality of American consumer products has also improved significantly. Capital spending is up and, since the 1981–83 recession, the economy has grown steadily, producing almost 12 million new jobs in the period January 1984 to December 1987. This is a 12 percent increase.

THE RESPONSE HAS BEEN INADEQUATE

In spite of this apparent progress, increases in productivity still lag behind that of many developed countries, and there is abundant evidence that American management is not viewed as competitive on a world scale. In the late 1980s, many years since the publication of "Managing Our Way to Economic Decline,"[4] numerous articles in reputable publications decry the state of American business management.

In the September–October 1987 issue of the *Harvard Business Review* there is a report of the results of a survey conducted by the *HBR* of its readers in May–June of 1987.[5] The purpose of the survey was to answer three groups of questions:

---

[4]Robert H. Hayes and William J. Abernathy, "Managing Our Way to Economic Decline," *Harvard Business Review* (July–August 1980). pp. 67–81.

[5]"Competitiveness Survey: HBR Readers Respond," *Harvard Business Review* (September–October 1987), p. 8–

- Is there a competitiveness problem? If so, how serious is it? How long has it been going on and how long will it continue?
- Who should shoulder the primary responsibility for the problem?
- Who should contribute the most to the solution?

The survey response shows the following:

- Ninety-two percent believe American competitiveness is *deteriorating*.
- Almost 90 percent believe the burden of responsibility is on the shoulders of U.S. managers.[6]
- Ninety-seven percent think the solution will come through more effective management.

It is worth noting that while the demographics of respondents to the survey was not identified in the survey report, the *HBR* states that 95 percent of its subscribers are in business, industry, or the professions; 82 percent are directly in management; and 42 percent are in top management. Presumably it is American managers who said American companies are becoming less competitive.[7] The facts in many markets here and abroad support this view.

BUSINESS AS USUAL

How can this be? In my view, the answer is quite simple. *The overwhelming majority of American companies are still using the same management system that got us into trouble in the first place.* For all our breast-beating and handwringing, changes American companies have made are the very ones managers using the traditional American management system can be expected to make. We were not trimming corporate staff and middle managers because we wanted to fundamentally change

---

[6]Many readers blamed other sources as well, such as the government and organized labor.

[7]"Subscriber Study," *Harvard Business Review* (Autumn 1986), p. 18.

the way we manage the corporation, but rather to reduce costs. What has changed is our willingness to do hard things such as reduce overhead and close unprofitable plants. Even the companies that have been restructured by outsiders are not managed in any fundamentally different way. Let us see why.

THE ANALOGUE MANAGEMENT TRAP

The modern American management system can be characterized as a system of concepts and tools intended to maximize the ability of the top management group to understand, direct, and control the business. At the heart of this system are two fundamental premises:

- The important characteristics of a business can be quantified.
- This ability to quantify can be used to directly support all the management activities (i.e., understanding, directing, and controlling the enterprise).

These two premises, as they are used in the American management system, are false and lead to a management style I call "Analogue Management" or managing through representations of reality. *In my view, this management style is at the heart of our competitiveness problem.*

The word *analogue* comes from analogy and means "to represent something with something else." Frequently, analogues are used as convenient measures of reality. For example, temperature is measured with a thermometer. The analogue gets its usefulness from the fact that there is agreement about the meaning of a specific reading. (The freezing point of water is equally well represented [analogued] by a thermometer reading of either 32° Fahrenheit or 0° Centigrade.) Use of analogues as measurement tools is ubiquitous in modern life. We use:

- Meters and liters to measure distance and volume.
- Grades to measure a student's performance.
- Points to measure compliance with the driving laws.

- Pencil-and-paper tests to measure personal attributes such as intelligence, aptitude, and personality.

Analogues are not reality, but merely a representation of that reality. Therefore, more than one approach may be used to analogue the same reality. Using a simple example of measuring temperature, there are many ways to build a thermometer. Some use columns of liquids, some expanding metal, and so forth. There can be, and are, a number of grading systems for students—letter grades and numeric systems are both used. Sometimes students are even graded for their level of effort and cooperation.

Because analogues are not the reality and because some things are much more difficult to represent or analogue than others, users of analogue measures must be very careful to understand the limits of the analogues they are using. In order to do this we need to understand the assumptions underlying the analogue because these assumptions are the basis from which the analogue gets its ability to represent the reality.

In the case of simple thermometers, one of the assumptions is that a certain material will expand and contract with some degree of uniformity as the temperature changes. Another assumption is that these changes are accurately represented by the readings on the particular type of thermometer. People, such as scientists, who need better accuracy than a particular thermometer can produce simply don't use it.

The use of analogues has become highly developed in the modern American management process. For understanding the business, businesses have analogues such as these:

- Income statements.
- Balance sheets.
- Product or service cost calculations.
- Profitability measures of subunits of the business such as Division, Location, Product line, Customer.
- Market share measurement.
- Sales forecasting models.
- Statistically based market research data.

For directing the business, analogues have been developed such as these:

- Profit or operating plans.
- Sales quotas.
- Spending budgets.
- Production schedules.
- Management by objective systems.
- Strategic plans.

For controlling the business actual results are reported against the analogues used for directing the business. In addition, other analogues are used for control, such as these:

- Statistical quality control techniques.
- Capital allocation using discounted cash-flow techniques.
- Job classifications.
- Spending authority limits.
- Performance evaluations.
- Incentive-compensation plans.

As vehicles for understanding the business, analogues can be quite useful. Especially as a business grows, the analogues enable managers to see more of the business. Among other things, they help managers understand sales, earnings, production, and the returns on potentially competing investments of limited capital. By enabling managers to compare the results of one period with those of another, analogues allow them to gauge progress.

The analogues have also been useful in reporting the results of a business entity's activities to outsiders: to current and prospective stockholders, to analysts, creditors, and tax authorities. Also, by bringing together so many disparate business activities into a common, easily understandable, numerical language, analogues allow managers to communicate effectively with managers in different areas within the organization.

Analogues have also proven useful as management control tools. Profit plans, for example, serve a motivational function, encouraging managers to perform better than they might without them. Spending budgets play an integral role in achieving planned profits and also can be helpful in executing cost reductions more thoughtfully and systematically. Hurdle rates can be used to communicate certain guidelines about the kinds of investments that are acceptable as well as about those that are not. Profit centers can help decentralize management, allowing teams of managers greater autonomy and room for innovation. A manager's compensation can be partly linked to some analogues of performance as an incentive to encourage the manager to work harder and/or with a specific focus he might otherwise not have.

The analogues that form the basis of modern management technology also play a major role in our current management problem. Our misuse of these analogues has created the current situation and is simultaneously the reason American companies seem unable to change. Like users of some powerful addictive drug, American companies have become dependent on a harmful management process that managers seem unable to stop using. Most are unable to withdraw from the system, even though many of them have come to understand its inherent dangers. I choose to call this phenomenon the *"analogue management trap."*

American companies fall into the analogue management trap by making three fundamental errors:

- Believing they can have analogued measurements of the businesses that are more comprehensive and more accurate than is actually possible.
- Believing they can control against analogued results and thereby effectively manage the underlying *business activities*.
- Not understanding that managing through analogues is self-fulfilling.

These misconceptions have inexorably drawn the management process, whether practiced inside or observed from outside, to focus on analogues when judging the success of the management process. Gradually, analogues have become the *only "valid"* measures. Because *managers believe they can manage using them,* that is what they attempt to do. Thus analogue management traps managers into investing their effort in areas valued by the analogues. As a result, those activities not valued by the analogues, many of which are in the company's long-term competitive interest, receive secondary attention. Let's expand on the three misconceptions at the heart of our problem.

MANAGERS BELIEVE THAT THE ANALOGUES MORE ACCURATELY REPRESENT THE REALITY OF THE BUSINESS THAN THEY ACTUALLY DO

A number of analogue measures of business exist, many of them based on the accounting system. Individually and as a group, these systems are not as accurate and comprehensive as many believe. Rather than use these measures as the limited resource they actually are, we treat them as being both absolutely true and, when taken together, a complete picture of the business. Of course, managers examine other information when engaged in the day-to-day management job, but achieved results are usually quantified by using an analogue.

This process has been carried so far that those attributes of a business which defy quantification have become almost unmanageable. Satisfying a customer's desire to change his order must be explained in terms of its effect on the production schedule. Fair enough one might say, but where is the analogue for customer satisfaction against which we measure the damage to the production schedule analogue? Equipment replacement decisions must frequently pass through a capital budgeting system wherein the rate of return on the investment must somehow be quantified. The decision is sometimes further complicated by the need to "write-off" the remaining undepreciated book value on the equipment being replaced. What if the proposed equipment is a response to a competitor's action and will only help hold market share? Where is the analogue representing the value of this market share in the capital budgeting formula? Is it really even possible to totally quantify this decision?

The most obvious example of this incompleteness and inaccuracy is the ability of the modern American accounting system to measure overall corporate performance. In fact, a business can be very profitable, as measured by the accounting system, and still unhealthy at the same time.

- American automobile companies had record profits in 1977 just as they were beginning to lose an additional 15 percent of the American market to foreign competitors.
- The Bank of America had record profits in 1980 when CEO Thomas Clauson left. Seven years later (most good years for the economy) it teetered on the brink of bankruptcy.
- Dozens of well-known companies have shown earnings and sales growth for years only to require restructuring as they are exposed as inefficient asset packages.

Since the phenomenon constantly occurs, one would think most companies would realize the inadequacies of our accounting system. In fact, all the evidence indicates that the opposite is true. Quarterly results are eagerly awaited and publicly reported. Accounting data are used in a number of off-line ways to measure aspects of the business such as product cost or customer profitability. However the most significant measure of our regard for accounting results as a measure of business success is the web of regulation and control surrounding the reporting of financial results to the public.

The federal government through the Securities and Exchange Commission has issued literally hundreds of regulations covering public reporting issues and thousands of interpretations of these regulations since it was founded in 1933. The public accounting profession through its Financial Accounting Standards Board (FASB) has also worked hard at defining what are called Generally Accepted Accounting Principles (GAAP). The securities laws require that the published financial results of the publicly held companies be audited against both these sets of rules.

Further, no self-respecting American company of any size operates without a financial plan. In many companies, this plan is not called a financial plan but rather an operating plan (as though the company makes money not products and services).

As will be seen in the next chapter, the accounting system is incapable of the task it has been given, and no amount of regulation or modification can fix it in any fundamental way. The fact that a major and apparently accelerating effort to do this continues, is a major reason I believe we are caught in an analogue management trap.

AMERICAN MANAGERS BELIEVE THEY CAN CONTROL AGAINST ANALOGUED RESULTS AND AS A RESULT, MANAGE THE UNDERLYING BUSINESS ACTIVITIES

A key unspoken assumption underlying the modern American management system is when you manage to a planned ana-logued result, the *underlying business activities have been properly managed.* It is easy to show how this is not necessarily the case. There are many methods to accomplish a monthly or annual profit plan that are actually mismanagement by any objective standard. Just because a departmental budget was not *overspent* does not mean it was *well* spent (or that the original budget was correct for that matter!). How many production schedules have been met by shipping faulty products?

If one looks beyond the short-range to other analogues such as the Corporate or Long-Range Plan the story is the same. Corporations frequently use a Corporate or Long-Range Plan to alter the strategic direction of the corporation. For example, they may choose to change the mix of their sales and profits from their mainline business in order to make them less volatile, less defense dependent, and so forth. Examples abound of companies blindly following these plans as if the economy rewards planning per se. The dismal results achieved by many of these companies, some of which are being restructured today, shows otherwise. *Achieving the planned objective does not automatically assure the planned result* (i.e., a stronger company).

In many ways the belief that management can "control" to an analogued result may be a bigger problem to the management process than managers' unchallenged faith in the accuracy of the analogues themselves. It is probably true that managing to an analogue not only fails to manage the underlying business activities but also *can damage the validity of the measures themselves.* If one tries to control the temperature of air by holding a thermometer in one's hand, one has simultaneously failed to control the temperature of the object being measured and destroyed the validity of the measurement itself. A measurement can only be accurate if the measurement system has not been interfered with. The more we manage to analogues, the less we can trust the reported results. Two dollars a share for a company managing the overall business and accepting the financial results that occur, is not the same as two dollars a share from a company that manages itself to earn two dollars a share.

MANAGING TO ANALOGUES IS SELF-FULFILLING

Perhaps the most insidious thing about managing to analogue measures is simply this—it works! If one sets out to tightly control a business against analogue targets, whether these targets are accounting measures, diversification plans, or the targets in an MBO program, the objectives tend to be achieved. Also it is usually clear that the results were achieved because the management process focused on achieving them.

I believe this is the mind-set that led American managers into the analogue trap in the first place. In an attempt to improve the management process, managers tried to ape the success of the physical sciences by appropriating their "scientific" technique. To many, that meant emphasizing a quantification of activities to allow for objective management.

An increasing emphasis on managing objective targets became popular and sure enough it seemed to work. When ambitious financial targets were set, companies tended to have higher profits. Higher growth targets naturally resulted in more rapid growth. Even managing individual executives to individual MBO programs seemed to work. Gradually, the management process evolved to emphasize the management of analogued results rather than the business itself. Business managers favored executives who were skilled analogue managers. Chief financial officers made more and more money, absolutely and relative to manufacturing executives. More accountants and lawyers became CEOs.

The difficulty was that, because of the inherent weakness that the analogues have, this did not mean that the businesses themselves were being better managed. Further, the analogue results began to be valued to the point where we progressed from manipulating management behavior to achieve our analogue goals, to manipulating the analogue systems themselves. While corporations had attempted to manipulate their published financial results for years, most people understood this was chicanery and it resulted in the Securities Acts of 1933 and 1934. These were the laws which created the SEC and the requirement for outside auditors.

However, a fine art has been developed for manipulating published results which depends on the particular transactions being within the rules. A rolling process has been created in which financial manipulation is "invented" and the SEC, FASB, and AICPA attempt to evaluate it in the context of the stated objective of accounting (i.e. to fairly present financial results). Approaches that are ruled improper are often replaced by a new generation of "innovative" techniques.

This type of behavior is no longer regarded as nefarious. It is taught in business schools and vigorously discussed in the business press and on Wall Street. American managers have come to *believe* their results to the point where anything that produces the desired results is as good as any other method.

This psychology also extends to internal management control reporting. Financial and nonfinancial targets are vigorously negotiated between superior and subordinate *as if they were working for different organizations*. There is much discussion about the rules of the road relative to how various issues will be handled in the reporting system. Executives frequently do things that are the micro equivalent of the corporation making profits from the "aggressive" use of the accounting rules; that is, they use approaches to improve their reported performance that are within the rules but are in fact a manipulation of the system.

What exists is a system that seems capable of producing the intended results and therefore seems to work as a way of managing the business. In fact, it is frequently self-fulfilling without necessarily producing the management results it *seems* to be causing and reporting.

STUCK IN THE ANALOGUE
MANAGEMENT TRAP

While many people recognize that the American management process produces unsatisfactory *outcomes*, they *have underestimated the difficulties associated with changing behavior*. Its important to remember:

- The current generation of American managers have "grown up" using the present management technology. It is the only system they know. Furthermore, they got where they are because they are good at using it.
- Much of American business is publicly held. The "public" ownership also has grown up understanding and believing the current management technology. They

may not like some current results but it is not clear (particularly to the managements of publicly held companies) that these outside owners are able or willing to understand significant shifts in management behavior.
- The American business intellectual community (business schools, business press, etc.) has so focused on the language and concepts of our present system that efforts in other directions often seem like "nonmanagement" both to managers themselves and those who observe their performance.

Because of these and similar other difficulties, the old management technology still has the "sophisticated high ground" in the American economy. The current situation is *not going to change until a critical mass of executives and members of the business intellectual community are more familiar with the false premises underlying our management system.*

This book is an attempt to do just that. The first part of the book focuses on the limitations of the analogue measures themselves and on the reality of what managing through them does to the management process and the individual managers involved. It is intended to help the individual manager, and those who observe his behavior, to better comprehend what the limitations of our analogue-based management system really are and how we have been trapped into using this system. This in turn should begin to help us *put analogues back into their rightful place in our management system based on a realistic understanding of what their role can be.* If the argument is persuasive, we will be more willing to accept the analogues for the limited measures they are and admit that we must learn the rest of what we want to know about a business some other way.

For example, American managers are accused of being too interested in short-run profits. For years the advice has been to tell them they should become more long-run oriented. While there is some truth to this accusation, it requires us to believe that managers are simultaneously unprincipled enough to deliberately sacrifice the future of their companies and stupid enough to stay with the very companies they are destroying. Further, it requires us to believe others would let managers do this and in fact reward them for doing so. A more plausible explanation would seem to be that, to the extent that striving for short-run profits is a problem (and it is), managers and others concerned with their performance *misunderstand* what is being measured by the accounting system and *overvalue* its ability to measure management performance.

Rather than advocate that management "trade" some profits for longer-run objectives such as market share, Chapter 2 attempts to expose (in nontechnical language) the actual technical limitations of the accounting system as a measurement tool, thereby giving a manager a *reason* to reduce his emphasis on its results based on insight into the reality of what the system can and cannot be used for as one attempts to manage a business. (Merely recommending that a manager reduce his emphasis on short-run accounting profits does not tell him either why or how much in a way that is directly usable, to say nothing of helping him explain his decision to others.)

Likewise, the other chapters in Part I are focused on dissecting our analogue management system and describing how it inexorably leads to the kind of management bias American managers are accused of having.

In order to free ourselves from the analogue management trap we must achieve understanding on four issues. We must understand:

- How incredibly inadequate analogues are as measures of a company's competitive viability, particularly as they measure this in a given time period.
- Managing against analogue targets is not the same as managing the underlying business activities and probably even affects the validity of the results reported against these targets.
- We are in the vicious cycle called the analogue trap.

- Managing the realities of the business such as the customers and products does not hurt but actually improves the results reported by the analogue measures, as we shall see.

Part II of the book is dedicated to offering suggestions on how to improve the management process in a company that is departing the "analogue management trap."

CHAPTER 2

THE AMERICAN ACCOUNTING SYSTEM—A BADLY FLAWED ANALOGUE

The American accounting system is the "King of the Analogues" in the American business management process. Through the balance sheet, it purports to portray the business at a point in time; through the income statement the results of the business over a given period of time.

Accounting transactions support other analogues used in the management process. Analogues such as product costs and location profitability calculations are relied on to better understand the business. Budget reports are created to control the business. Furthermore, American business takes accounting system outputs quite seriously.

Externally, the income statement and balance sheet, clothed in their wrappers of regulations, standards, and a "clean" audit opinion, are examined carefully by a number of constituencies including security analysts, lenders, business journalists, and current and potential investors. Comparisons of year-to-year, and even quarter-to-quarter, results are made. Ratios are frequently computed to allow investors, lenders, and others interested in more detail, to understand what has been reported. Much is made of relatively small (for example 10 percent) changes in reported earnings. Broad terms such as *turnaround* are used to characterize a current year's increase in profits from a loss or poor profits in the previous year, often even when the previous year's profits were depressed by a "write-off."

Internally the managers are if anything even more focused on accounting system outputs. There is obviously the matter of managing the results that will be reported to the public. However, the internal management analogues that use accounting data are also important. Products are dropped or their prices raised when the reported product costs make them unprofitable at their current price. Profit center managers receive bonuses based on reported profits. Managers are promoted or transferred. Locations are expanded or closed and so forth.

OUR GREAT EXPECTATION

Unfortunately, the accounting system is a very imperfect measure of corporate performance. It simply cannot technically meet our expectations with any degree of precision.

To understand why the accounting system cannot meet our expectations, it is helpful to use the suggestion in Chapter 1 and review the assumptions on which it is based. There are in fact two:

- If a financial transaction does not take place, then nothing really occurs in the business.
- If a financial transaction occurs, then what happened in the business is properly portrayed by the accounting system.

To the extent that these two assumptions are at variance with the realities of the business, the accounting system loses accuracy as a true representation of the business.

In fact, both of these assumptions are highly unrealistic. Business is a collection of activities carried out by people. Some activities create a financial transaction and some do not. To the extent an activity creates a financial transaction, the accounting system may or may not be able to process it properly. In order to illustrate these points, let's examine each of the assumptions as they are used to portray the company's performance to outsiders through balance sheets and income statements.

Let's start with the assumption requiring a financial transaction. On the surface, this is a reasonable assumption. The accounting system, by definition, requires transactions to be denominated in monetary terms. In practice, however, this assumption causes several real business events to go unrecorded and, therefore, unrecognized. These events include the following:

- Failure to maintain physical assets. (The accounting system, in fact, penalizes maintenance by reducing profits, while rewarding a lack of maintenance with profit increases.)
- Failure to preserve, let alone enhance, other "real" corporate assets. These include some of the company's most important assets such as the product portfolio, distribution system, human organization, and technological base.
- Losses of market position or market share.
- Activities that consciously or unwittingly serve to downgrade or jeopardize product quality.
- An increase, as a result of inflation or other factors, in the replacement cost of the equipment that is used in the business.
- Technological change that makes equipment that is still physically useful less economically valuable.

In the mid-1970s Control Data Corporation was the only manufacturer of super computers on the planet. During this time Seymour Cray, its top engineer, and a number of other engineers left the company. On that day, assuming no financial settlements were made, the accounting system said "nothing happened." At the present time, Control Data has left the super computer market and Cray Research, the company founded by these men, holds over 70 percent of the super computer market. Said another way, because it must of necessity ignore these and similar business phenomena, the accounting system is in effect assuming that management is doing the right thing in the areas it cannot "see" and measuring its performance on that basis.

The second assumption, if a financial transaction occurs the accounting system portrays it properly, requires us to believe that the accounting system can convert any financial transaction to a reasonable representation of its business reality. In many cases, this obviously is not true. A good illustration is how the system decides whether to capitalize a transaction (recognize an expenditure as creating an asset) or to treat the expenditure as a current period expense.

According to Generally Accepted Accounting Principles (GAAP), a transaction should be recorded as a current period expense unless a tangible, measurable asset is created. It follows from this rule that expenses incurred in connection with purchasing or building a product for sale (inventory), and with purchasing plant equipment are capitalized. The system can also capitalize exchanging an asset for an asset such as when inventory is sold and an account receivable is created. *However, expenses incurred in connection with the preservation or enhancement of less tangible assets must be expensed.* Less tangible assets include, in this case, corporate "assets" recognized as real but that are not accounts receivable, inventory, or plant and equipment. These assets include:

- Reputation for product quality.
- Competitive market position.
- Distribution system.
- Product portfolio.
- Technological base.
- Human organization.

Even this cursory look at the accounting system indicates that its underlying assumptions deviate from the reality of business in very serious ways. More importantly, these deviations tend to cluster in the areas of business activity related to building or preserving the company's long-term assets—

whether these assets are on the balance sheet, such as plant and equipment, or off the balance sheet, such as the company's human organization or its market position.

Further, *the accounting rules create a consistent bias in the system toward short-run behavior.* They always fail to capitalize, thereby undervalue, expenses incurred to enhance assets that the system cannot quantify, such as the market position or the quality of the organization. Meanwhile, the rules do not allow the system to recognize that management has failed to maintain these same assets, or for that matter its physical, balance-sheet assets such as plant and equipment.

The effect of this bias is to understate the costs and, therefore, *overstate the profits of companies that do not maintain all their assets.* Conversely, the bias serves to *understate the profits of companies* creating off-balance-sheet assets. Both these distortions are much more serious than they might seem at first glance.

Consider, for example, that after all costs, most companies earn less than 10 percent on sales. That means that over 90 percent of revenue is consumed by the cost of operating the company. Understating the costs of most businesses by 10 percent will more than double their bottom-line profit.

This issue exceeds the boundaries of simple bookkeeping. Overstating profits will, in almost all cases, cause a company to lose cash. A company with a marginal federal and state income tax rate of 40 percent and a dividend of 30 percent of after-tax profits will send about 58 percent of every overstated dollar permanently out of the business as cash.[1]

One hears the argument frequently that the system "catches up with itself." That is, if the current year's profits are overstated because the system fails to recognize that an asset, particularly a "off-balance" asset such as the company's

---

[1]Taxes $\quad = \quad 1.00 \quad \times .40 = \$.40$
Dividend $= (1.00 - .40) \quad \times .3 \quad = \underline{\quad.18}$
$$\$.58$$

market position, has been diminished, the accounting system will correct itself by reporting lower profits in future years, as the consequences of the diminished market position are realized through lower sales. The only truth in this argument is that future profits, as they are reported by the accounting system, will probably be lower.

The unspoken conclusion that there is nothing to worry about is not true. First, no matter what occurs, the company's cash is gone. The resource needed to rebuild on-balance-sheet or off-balance-sheet assets has been permanently reduced. A write-off to adjust the books does not produce cash. Secondly, the accounting system reports these results too late and too imprecisely. It is too late because managers are trying to manage in the current period. It is too imprecise because there are just too many questions that still cannot be answered accurately. How much of the current period's result relates to past failures? To what past period can the problems be traced? How far into the future will past overstatements affect profits? In what period? By how much? It is important to bear in mind that we are dealing with damaged assets. In fact, the accounting system faces increased problems as the time period measured gets shorter.

THE TIME PERIOD PROBLEM

As we have seen, the most glaring problem with the accounting system is its inability to account properly for the company's assets. This trouble exists whether these assets are on-balance-sheet or off-balance-sheet assets. As a result, the accounting system becomes a less precise analogue of the real economic results of a business as the time period shortens.

In the normal operation of a business, daily investments are made in the company's on-balance-sheet and off-balance-sheet assets. In addition, previous asset building makes a contribution daily to management's ability to operate the business. The process of investing and experiencing the benefits of these investments is heavily overlapped. Thus, the results experienced in any time period are a mixture of the management's current actions and the results of investments made in previous time periods. The result of management's actions in the present time period are, to some degree, expressed as investments made for subsequent periods.

A SMALL BUSINESS ACCOUNTING DILEMMA

Let's illustrate this process with a simplified example of a single entrepreneur opening a small retail store in a large mall. In the first month our entrepreneur invests in some fixtures and inventory both of which are recorded by his accounting system as assets. He also invests in training an organization of two or three employees, an advertisement in a local paper, and in customer goodwill by accepting returned merchandise that is not defective. None of these latter investments are recorded as assets and, it can be argued, were all recorded in the accounting system as current period costs.

In the second month, while continuing to make both on-balance-sheet and off-balance-sheet investments, our entrepreneur also receives returns on some (but not necessarily all) of the investments he made in the first month. Perhaps some customers come in because they have seen the advertisement or perhaps because the customer who returned the goods has recommended the store. In all probability, the accounting system will show a bigger profit (or more likely a smaller loss) in the second month than in the first. Is this true economically? The second month is clearly benefiting from the first. Management activity and another month on the site (represented in the accounting system as a lease payment and other "fixed" expenses in month two) will contribute to the revenues in month three. So what really happened, economically speaking, in month two? Clearly something other than what is represented in the accounting system.

Our entrepreneur may now decide to liquefy some or all of his off-balance-sheet assets. For example, he could do this by taking a partner who will pay more than book value for the share of the business he gets for his investment. This possibility shows that in the mind of the investor, the accounting system never caught up with the economic reality of the business. However, who would say that the investor can rely on the fact that the company's assets are understated on the balance sheet? Clearly the opposite of the start-up may be occurring. The company, perhaps now much larger and in several malls, may be suffering from "management problems" which have not yet expressed themselves in the reported results. These so-called "management problems" in reality represent management's failure to maintain their on- and off-balance-sheet assets.

In larger more complex companies, the short-run results are even less meaningful. A large company's current period results are the product of the company's momentum combined with short-term circumstances. *At the monthly or quarterly level, they are almost meaningless as a measure of management performance. On an annual basis they are only marginally better.*

If the company is a manufacturing company, the following are true:

- It is selling products that were designed (and the design paid for) in previous accounting periods.
- The physical assets, even those put in service in the current period, are the result of management decisions made in previous periods.
- The human organization, distribution system, and competitive market position have likewise been built over the years.
- The positions of the company's various products in their "life cycles" have a lot to do with their saleability but are hardly the results of current period management actions.

However, for most managers it seems necessary to manage the business vigorously on a day-to-day basis. Because reported profits actually fluctuate significantly from month to month or quarter to quarter, many believers in the analogued results are convinced that the game is really a short-term affair. In fact, a built-in volatility exists in the reporting of profits adding to the system's already serious problem of measuring short-run performance rather than being evidence that *real* corporate performance is significantly changing. This volatility is largely a product of the high percentage of fixed costs at most large companies. (Fixed costs are those costs that do not fluctuate in the short run with changes in sales volume.) Small changes in sales volumes, in companies with significant fixed costs, can cause large changes in reported profits. Furthermore, in companies with significant fixed costs, small changes in the level of the fixed costs have the same multiplier effect.[2]

For example, if a company's profits are 5 percent of sales and fixed costs are 50 percent of all costs, a 1 percent increase in sales will increase profits slightly more than 10 percent.[3] Similarly, a 1 percent change in fixed cost can produce a slightly less than 10 percent change in profits.[4] Clearly, doing 1 percent better in one component of the business is not the same as managing the overall business 10 percent better as the reported profits seem to be saying.

Sustainable changes in a company's competitive position, even given today's shortening product life cycles, takes two to five years or more to achieve. It takes management that long to permanently affect the underlying assets that are the drivers of the costs and revenues reported by the accounting system.

---

[2]For reasons which will be discussed later, it is also much easier to reduce "fixed" costs than it is to reduce costs that vary with the level of sales.

[3]$1.00 Sales	$1.01
.475 Var. Cost	.47975
.525 Gross Margin	.53025
.475 Fixed Costs	.475
$ .05 Profit	$.05525

[4]$1.00 Sales	$1.00
.475 Var. Cost	.475
.525 Gross Margin	.525
.475 Fixed Cost	.47025
$ .05 Profit	$ .05475

It is particularly important that management focus on the maintenance and enhancement of its assets, especially the off-balance-sheet assets such as the quality of the human organization and the company's market position. Yet, as we have seen, the accounting system's ability to analogue this behavior in the short run is in fact minimal.

As the time period lengthens, the analogue is more accurate. Therefore, if a company has been profitable for, say, five years, that would be more meaningful than if the period were one year. However, because of the length of the investment cycle (i.e., the period between the time an investment in either on-balance-sheet or off-balance-sheet assets is made and the return from this investment is either successfully or unsuccessfully received) the closer one gets to the present the less these results will mean.

Therefore, even if a company has been profitable for several years, one cannot be certain that this success will continue even one more year. Management may have been underinvesting or making poor investments, particularly in off-balance-sheet assets, for three or four years and the results of this bad management may be about to appear as lower earnings. Conversely, a company may be about to show good earnings even though it has a poor history of doing so.

THE ASSUMPTIONS ARE NOT A SECRET

Before unduly condemning the accounting system, it is important to recognize that the rules were made not to bias the system but to enable it to function as unambiguously as possible. Every attempt was made to remove human judgment, and therefore bias, from the recording and classifying of transactions. The rules are public knowledge. The problem stems from our use of the system's results. Investors, lenders, business academics, business journalists, and regulators have invested more value in the reported results than they deserve.

In our eagerness to have one system serve as a gauge of our business performance, *we have imposed an impossible burden on the accounting system and have stopped asking whether what we are trying to achieve is really possible.* When the system's results surprise its users, when they notice that the underlying business realities do not follow their analogue representation, the users tend to react by suing the outside auditors or by seriously questioning whether accounting standards should be set by the government rather than the Financial Accounting Standards Board.

THE ROLE OF THE ACCOUNTING SYSTEM IN THE INTERNAL MANAGEMENT PROCESS

Up to this point, we have focused on the limitations of the accounting system to analyze overall corporate performance to outsiders. As we have seen, it is a severely limited analogue in this context and becomes less accurate when measuring shorter periods. All analysis of income-statement and balance-sheet data starts within these limitations and therefore cannot transcend them.

In spite of these obvious limitations the accounting system is the central analogue used in the short-run management of the modern American corporation. Almost every well-managed corporation uses an annual financial plan. This plan in reality, is the target income statement for year-end. (The balance sheet, though planned, receives less attention in most companies.)

The planned income statement is separated into its revenue and expense components and assigned by responsibility throughout the organization. In most organizations the revenue line becomes the responsibility of the Vice President of Sales. The various cost elements of the income statement become the spending budgets of all the vice presidents (including, of course, the Vice President of Sales who controls much of the selling expense). The financial plan is then calendarized into a monthly plan. These monthly plans are the targets against which the actual management takes place.

In order to accomplish their part of the plan, each vice president then allocates his target to the various components of his organization. The Vice President of Sales creates sales targets or quotas for the various aspects of revenue for each of the parts of his organization. All vice presidents allocate their expense budgets to the various previously defined "cost centers" in their organizations.

So there we have it! An airtight system. If every manager meets or beats his or her revenue or expense target the corporation automatically meets or beats its annual plan. Achieving the annual plan produces a satisfactory or better-than-satisfactory result, and by definition, the corporation has a successful year.

To ensure the plan is being accomplished, most corporations carefully control against it on a monthly basis. A detailed monthly "package" is prepared for senior management which allows them to evaluate overall corporate performance. Depending on the company, the "package" gives them an inside view into the various functional areas in some detail. However, regardless of the package's contents, each vice president is expected to maintain enough detailed information about his department to explain his organization's performance. To further assure that the financial plan will be met, many corporations create incentive-compensation systems. These systems encourage top management, and often middle management as well, to meet their own and the company's financial targets.

This ubiquitous management against a financial plan is a classic example of the "Analogue Management Trap":

- An analogue (the financial system) that "everybody" agrees measures something[5] much better than it really does.

---

[5]In this case the performance of a corporation and its management in a monthly, quarterly or annual time period.

- People within the corporation vigorously controlling against it and outsiders taking the results very seriously.
- The controls frequently producing the results we want.

In the next chapter we will discuss how the phenomenon of analogue management actually affects the management of American corporations.

CHAPTER 3

THE EFFECT OF ANALOGUE MANAGEMENT ON AMERICAN CORPORATIONS

This chapter is intended to characterize the effect of analogue management on American corporations. There are seven topics. They are the effect on:

- Top management behavior.
- The value-creation process.
- Departmental cooperation.
- Corporate nimbleness.
- Corporate viewpoint.
- The compensation process.
- Individual executives.

ANALOGUE MANAGEMENT REINFORCES THE IDEA THAT TOP MANAGEMENT CAN REALLY IMPACT SHORT-RUN ACTIVITIES

The American management system is characterized by a "top-down" orientation. Most executives believe that *competitive wisdom exists at the "top." The real challenge, from their perspective, is to motivate the organization to follow top management's lead.* Steven Brandt's well-known book[1] on the

---

[1]Steven C. Brandt, *Strategic Planning In Emerging Companies* (Reading, MA: Addison-Westley 1981)

crisis of management in growing companies clearly illustrates this point. Brandt postulates that as a small business prospers and grows it reaches a point where the original entrepreneur begins to lose control. His solution suggests that the company must begin to functionalize its organizational structure by creating specialized departments such as sales and manufacturing. Later, when the company has a full set of functionalized departments, it can divisionalize and so forth.

This concept in and of itself is not wrong. However, we need to question the role of top management as it creates this increasingly elaborate organizational structure. Specifically, how much *short-run control can top management expect to exercise*? Common sense would seem to indicate that the role of top management should become increasingly long-term oriented as its day-to-day management duties are assumed by lower level managers. How could it be otherwise? However, when managers believe they have accurate reporting systems on the operation, they can believe they have the ability to control short-run operations. Monthly reporting of profitability and other analogue data from a company's various operations provide top management with this sense of short-term control.

In fact, this sense of having short-run control exists throughout American industry and was perhaps epitomized by Harold Geneen's management of ITT. Geneen's approach was to have a monthly meeting attended by the heads of ITT's various business units. During this meeting the performance of each unit was reviewed using data that each unit had to submit in advance. Geneen was convinced that by monitoring each unit month by month he could actually understand and seriously influence their performance throughout the year. Because most executives don't question the validity of their analogue measures, their belief in top-down, short run management and that Mr. Geneen was right is reinforced.

Frequently one can connect bold action by top management to apparent short-run improvement in business results as measured by the analogues. It can seem all that was necessary to "straighten things out" was the desire of top management to "do something." Many times after a change in top management of a company occurs, due to poor results, we see a rapid improvement in profits in the next year or two. This frequently occurring scenario happens when the new management cuts fixed[2] costs vigorously in the first year. This cost cutting is frequently accompanied by write-downs of a number of assets, particularly inventories. These write-downs are justified by the need to recognize problems presumably unrecognized by the previous management as they attempted to maintain reported profitability.

The result in the transition year is sharply lower profits or even losses. These results are "understandable" and therefore regarded as good for the future. Profits improve sharply in the following year, particularly on a comparative basis. To an observer, it seems top management has taken bold action in turning the company around.

In fact, as was pointed out in Chapter 2, it is relatively simple to significantly change reported profits in the short run without a corresponding improvement in the corporation's competitive viability. Relatively small cuts in fixed costs can have a magnified impact on profits. The sale of previously written-down inventories, even at reduced prices can have an enormous one-time effect, as most managers well know.

In the real world of management, lasting improvements in companies of any size require a number of years to mature to the place where the improvement is significant and long-lasting. While these improvements are being accomplished out of necessity, top management needs to stimulate lower level management, who in turn must take the actions to actually improve the company. As we have seen, this process cannot be accurately analogued by the accounting system. In fact, you often hear managers engaged in fundamental improvement programs, whether at the company level or in a

---

[2]Variable costs, as we have suggested, are much more difficult to reduce.

lower level profit center, talk of feeding enough profit to the "outside world" to keep it at bay while continuing the real work of improving operations.

Much of the fabled "short-run orientation" of American managers is due to the belief that analogues, particularly the accounting system, are valid measures of short-run performance. Since these measures can be affected by top management in the short run, short-run management must work. Long-term oriented management behavior tends to do little to improve the analogue measures, and, can have negative short-run effects. As a result, long-run management tends to be neglected.

In my experience, the priority between the long and short term is that top management is prepared to do what it can about the long run as long as positive, short-run analogued results are achieved. If short-run results are in jeopardy, then the long-term priorities are often neglected until short-run issues are resolved.

ANALOGUE MANAGEMENT BIASES THE VALUE-CREATION PROCESS AWAY FROM CORPORATE ASSETS NOT FOUND ON THE BALANCE SHEET

Management can be defined as the act of deploying company resources to create value. The more value created, the better the management.

Viewed from the usual financial perspective, the company's cash is traded to vendors and employees for material and services that are combined to create the company's products and services. The use of noncash assets such as facilities and equipment is viewed as using "stored" cash expenditures over the productive life of these assets. The value created is "stored" as cash or some other asset such as accounts receivable or is used to reduce a liability. Management and the board of directors decide whether to keep the created value within the company for future use or transfer it to the stockholders in the form of dividends.

This financially based view of the value-creation process ignores those assets that are not trapped by the accounting system. *In fact, as management strives to create value, it trades away and stores created value in the nonbalance-sheet assets as well.* The company's market position, product portfolio, distribution system, and human organization along with the other off-balance-sheet assets all participate in the value-creation process. *It is the failure to properly evaluate these off-balance-sheet asset trades that is the essence of this criticism.*

When top management focuses on short-run financial results, the off-balance-sheet assets will experience two problems. The first problem is that improvements in off-balance-sheet assets will be undervalued because they are almost invisible to management in the short term. These assets do not appear in the regular accounting reports and cannot be easily quantified. The second problem is that any effort to add these assets, which creates a financial transaction, normally is recorded by the accounting system as a current period cost, not an investment.

Is it any wonder then that off-balance-sheet assets do not get a fair treatment by management? The following things are easy to do:

- Trade market share for short-run profits with a price increase.
- Depreciate the company's product portfolio by not investing in product development.
- Not enhance the company's ability to sell in markets that will require current expenditures on distribution networks, for example in foreign countries, which will only possibly produce sales in future periods.
- Neglect the company's human organization by promoting managers who "use up" their human resources as they "make their number" rather than those who build the company's human-resource base by making their results in a balanced way.

In fact, the neglect of off-balance-sheet assets such as these by American managers is the focus of the current criticism of them.

ANALOGUE MANAGEMENT HURTS THE ABILITY OF INDIVIDUAL DEPARTMENTS TO COOPERATE IN THE CORPORATION'S BEST INTEREST

The modern American corporation operates against a financial plan. If the company has divisions or other "business units," these are frequently treated as "profit" centers and have their own annual financial plan. As we have seen, the essence of controlling against a financial plan is to assign the responsibility for revenue and expenses to the various functional elements of the organization such as sales, manufacturing, engineering, and so forth. In addition to their revenue or costs targets the various functional units also have other analogue measures against which they are controlled. Performance against these analogue measures when taken together tends to be the measure of functional performance. Therefore, the system encourages managers to focus on the performance of their functional activity.

What is inherently wrong with this approach? For example, shouldn't sales executives focus on sales performance measures? *The problem with this approach is the consistent bias in these functional measures that favors departmental operations at the expense of the overall company, the customer, or both.* For example, sales volume has a natural conflict with margins, inventory levels, and manufacturing stability. Manufacturing costs have a natural conflict with responsiveness to the customer and the recognition of technologically obsolete equipment.

The problem extends to the divisional level as well. If a company has divisions or other profit centers that do business with each other, the supplying divisions want high transfer prices and the receiving divisions obviously want low ones. This leads divisions to buy material and services outside the corporation while there is capacity (and associated fixed cost) within the company. Conversely, supplying divisions may be reluctant to supply other divisions when they are short of capacity and can sell their valuable services to more profitable customers outside of the company.

In fact, the belief in analogue measures and in the ability to control effectively the underlying business activities through them, *results in a management strategy that attempts to maximize the total enterprise by maximizing the performance of the individual divisional units and the functional units within them.*

Many managers will argue that competition between various functional areas is healthy and achieves a balance between such issues such as long stable production runs and timely response to customers. Realistically managers competing blindly within a company through the use of crude performance measures is a poor method for balancing functional areas in light of the company's true needs. *Attempting to solve this never-ending problem is the real operational job of top management in larger organizations.* Doing this job with simplistic analogue controls is naive at best.

ANALOGUE MANAGEMENT HAS MADE AMERICAN CORPORATIONS LESS NIMBLE

American companies have a reputation for not being nimble, particularly when compared to other companies around the world. For example, American companies take almost twice as long to introduce new products as Japanese companies. Yet, one would think that a company with a top-down management orientation would be very nimble and therefore able to quickly make changes. After all, top management is closely involved in day-to-day operations, isn't it? In fact, top management of American corporations is interested in the *results* of short-term orientation as reported by the accounting system and other analogue measures but is not typically involved in *actual* operations.

Senior executives express interest in results through layers of middle managers and a large corporate staff. Middle managers are there to be sure plans are met. The staff exists to assist the line in meeting its objectives, or in some cases, to see that line management makes its plan without violating the corporation's rules.

The American management system runs under the unspoken assumption that we already know what to do, the problem is to get the organization to try hard enough to get the job done. Therefore, once we have decided what to do, every change must be evaluated in terms of its effect on the corporation's ability to make the plan if the proposed change is accommodated. Clearly the best way to accomplish change under this system is to include the consequences of the change in the planning process.

However, the annual planning process in most large American corporations usually spans several months. The finished version is sent to the board of directors at least one or two months before the year begins. Once the year starts, the problem of accommodating change occurs in the context of the corporate plan in each individual department. The problem must be defeated not just once but several times to accommodate each department's need to make its individual budgets, schedules, MBOs, and other analogue measures of performance. Many of these measures are tied to compensation either directly through incentive systems or indirectly as the performance measures of individual executives.

Contending with the corporate plan is just one of the problems in effecting rapid change in American corporations. There are several others. One is the whole process through which the modern American corporation decides to execute a change in the first place.

The corporate-level approval process is intended to ensure the effect of the change is fully understood before approval is given. Because the centrally planned corporation[3] doesn't like surprises, a number of processes are designed to analogue the results of a change before it is actually made. This is true for:

- A new product design.
- An organizational change.

---

[3]"Large American Corporations and Communist Societies Are Centrally Planned," Ken Olsen, CEO, Digital Equipment Corporation, Commencement Address, MIT, Spring 1987.

- A capital expenditure for plant or equipment.
- A decision to enter a new market.

These processes include:

- Capital budgeting systems with hurdle rates that an investment must be able to earn before it can even be considered in the system.
- Elaborate job-classification systems within which organizational changes are required to be placed.
- Staff reviews and or approvals of almost anything a line organization may wish to do. The usual justification for these reviews is that they are intended to protect the change makers and therefore the corporation from any lack of expertise the line managers may have. This missing expertise could be anything from technical knowledge such as legal, to the effects of the proposed change on other parts of the organization.

These processes create problems such as:

- Trading the time the process takes as if it had no cost (i.e. the process is so good, the time required is always justified). (The affect of time lag on a decision is almost impossible to analogue.)
- Requiring the change maker to justify the proposed change with analogue measurements which can be very difficult to do well.

How does one really quantify the return on an investment without knowing the probabilities associated with things such as competitor activity? How does one justify that a product-design characteristic cannot be removed without hurting net revenue more than the costs that are saved? When does it become absolutely necessary to replace a product or piece of capital equipment? If overemphasized as we are postulating, the approval process and the time it takes and the value of any help it can be, take on a cost that would never be paid if these services were offered in the open market rather than imposed as an internal requirement.

Review activities are not only overvalued but also involve some of the corporations' highest paying jobs and therefore attract some of the best people. Since the processes frequently involve negotiations between the staff who own the reviewing systems and the line managers who must pass through them, this talent imbalance can further bias the system toward delay and inertia. It also leads to the often-criticized practice of spreading responsibility for making a decision among so many executives that no one is really responsible for the final result.

ANALOGUE MANAGEMENT HAS MADE CORPORATIONS INWARD-LOOKING

There are many reasons for a management team to look beyond the corporation. *One can argue that everything that drives internal behavior starts with changes in the world outside the corporation.* Customers' desires and actual needs are constantly changing and must be monitored. The actions of competitors as they jockey for advantage must be known, understood, and evaluated. Almost every company has a regulatory environment with which it must also deal. Ignoring this regulatory process can be painful, as many companies have discovered. Technological change relevant to an individual company usually, at least, begins outside of it. Finally, under it all, there are those changes in the overall society in which the company operates. These changes affect the company directly in terms of such things as worker attitudes, but also drive much of what is perceived as changes in customer preference or the regulatory environment.

Phenomena such as these are difficult to analogue. They are particularly hard to analogue with the precision of a company's financial plan and other well-settled analogue measures such as production and product development schedules. Many companies manage to the internal analogues despite rapid changes in the external environment. As a result, the American manager has developed an inward-looking bias. He sees the need to focus on inwardly generated signals to change, viewing outside signals as being less valuable.

The advent of long-range (corporate) planning and strategic management tools far from changing this tendency, have intensified it. Long-range plans create the illusion that the outside world has been considered and is now represented in the internal analogue systems.

It is easy to find examples of companies and even whole industries that regarded themselves as sophisticated and yet were "blindsided" by changes in their outside environment. Most, if not all, of these changes were visible in plenty of time for proper preemptive action. Further, in many cases, these same companies were slow to react, even after they were aware of changes.

The much criticized automobile industry seemed equally puzzled by changing worker attitudes, safety legislation, and the Japanese strategy of competing with quality. Each of these problems took years to actually become significant. The consumer electronics industry could not have been blind to the technological changes that had the potential of sharply reducing the cost of electronic devices and making a whole range of new consumer products feasible. Could it be that by focusing on day-to-day operations, which were much more adequately analogued, these companies missed an expansion opportunity most industries would have been eager to exploit and simultaneously misunderstood the threat from Japan?

Operating against a financial plan is particularly insidious in its effect on the outward-looking process. Because companies are organized into functional organizations, it is these organizations that are doing most of the outside observing when it does occur. Sales sees changing customer needs. Engineering is aware of technological change. Manufacturing learns new manufacturing options.

Unfortunately, in the competitive race for a larger piece of a corporate budget, there is no simple way to translate the knowledge gained into corporate action. It is in the short-run interest of each functional unit to downplay the importance of the insight being claimed by the other functional units to the extent this would cause additional spending (really investment) by those other units.

ANALOGUE MANAGEMENT FOSTERS THE CREATION OF INCENTIVE-COMPENSATION SYSTEMS THAT ARE NAIVE AND OFTEN COUNTERPRODUCTIVE

The use of incentive compensation, whether piecework rates on a factory floor or bonuses for top executives, is obviously based on the idea of aligning the goals of the individual employee with those of the corporation. The intent is to achieve more effective work from the employee than could otherwise be expected. Enough additional output, in fact, to exceed the additional compensation paid.

Incentive-compensation systems used in the analogue management environment of most American corporations have the exact opposite effect. These systems actually work to further separate the goals of the individual executives from those of the corporation for two simple reasons:

- Such systems are based on analogue measures of the business. This reinforces the legitimacy of those measures and consequently increases the distortion produced in the management process.
- The incentive systems themselves, as they attempt to translate the analogue outputs into compensation in an "objective" fashion, introduce a further level of distortion into the process.

The Legitimacy of Analogue Measures Is Reenforced

Even in an environment where "analogue management" is practiced, an executive can operate in the company's interest to the detriment of his analogue measures and still have some hope of being rewarded. Presumably even the most analogue-oriented superior can be reasoned with, at least some of the time. However, once executives are "hard-wired" to the analogues, this becomes much more difficult. Situations can exist where executives must reduce their own bonus to act in the corporation's best interest. This process can be quite insidious. As the analogues persistently favor the short run over the longer run, the process can require executives to be quite heroic, on the one hand, while not requiring them to be very "sinful," on the other.

For example, to favor the short-run analogue results for a quarter or even a year may not disastrously or even definitely cripple the long-run interests of the enterprise. A price increase to cover a noncompetitive cost structure doesn't necessarily cost market share in the short run, but a failure to raise prices will certainly show up in the short-term results. Superior product reputations can survive long after they are deserved and the entire issue is difficult to measure objectively. Meanwhile, the effect on the short-run results of a raise in product-development expense is certain and the amount predictable.

Further, the legitimacy of the analogue measures have been reenforced, encouraging "analogue management" as a management style. What could be more normal for senior executives who are "hard wired" to analogue results than to pass these targets down through the organization and focus lower level managers on their attainment. After all, it's money in their pockets. As managers collect the money they will normally be praised for good performance both within the corporation and outside of it.

The Compensation System Itself Further Distorts Management Behavior

The use of incentive-compensation systems as a device for aligning the objectives of individual executives with those of the corporation not only depends on the validity of the corporate analogue measures being used, *it also relies on the technical validity of the compensation system itself.* A system must be constructed that translates corporate analogued results to another level of abstraction (i.e., "fair" incentive compensations to dozens or even thousands of individuals). To accomplish this task the compensation system must solve at least four major problems:

- Determining which executives (employees) are eligible for incentive compensation.

- Determining which corporate analogues to use.
- Determining how to translate various levels of "performance" as measured by these analogues into the total bonus pool (or pools).
- Determining how to distribute the pool to the participants.

A conflict also exists between the desire to create a system that is truly mechanical and the technical problems that must be solved to create such a system. Those who favor a more mechanical system are trying to make the system more "objective" by limiting the "judgement" which can be exercised by the executives who manage the compensation process. In practice, it is very difficult to predict all the business circumstances that can occur, let alone analogue the results that will be produced and used for incentive-compensation purposes.

The effect of all of this in many cases is to inadvertently create a game within the game of making one's numbers. In this second game the objective is to make one's numbers in the way most favored by the incentive-compensation system, since it cannot be relied upon to do this properly or because there are ways of "beating" the system.

ANALOGUE MANAGEMENT HAS A NEGATIVE EFFECT ON THE PERFORMANCE, DEVELOPMENT, AND ATTITUDES OF MANY INDIVIDUAL MANAGERS

Analogue management can also have profound negative effects on the individual manager who must use it. These effects include:

- Difficulty in maturing professionally.
- Loss of control of the activities for which they are responsible (believe it or not!).
- Difficulty in acting in the company's best interest as they see it.
- The creation of a success pattern that favors self-oriented rather than company-oriented executives.

Difficulty in Maturing Professionally

As the managers focus more and more on "making their numbers," they have a tendency to focus on those activities of their subordinates that most directly affect these measurements. Because of the inadequacy of analogues, these may not be the most important things for them to be worrying about. As a result, managers may be subtly taking themselves out of the flow of the real business by seeing and managing their organizations in a very narrow context.

Most of the insight and leadership a manager has comes from a *personal ability to understand what the organization actually does and how it does it.* This ability and knowledge is used to make choices and guide subordinates' behavior. This activity feeds back more knowledge and influence and allows the manager to "stay on top" of his or her job.

To the extent managers overfocus on the analogued results of their unit's activity, they will fail to get the feedback from those aspects of its work that they are ignoring. Gradually they will fail to appreciate or, if new to the job, fail to learn the full consequences of the various decisions they are making. Because they only see part of the picture clearly, their decisions tend to be biased toward what they understand (i.e., the analogue effect). Like the color-blind person who sees the pattern of a tie more clearly than its color, they have difficulty making proper choices. Their development is actually regressing. As they are promoted and get farther from the actual work, this situation is exacerbated.

Analogue Management Can Lead to Less Actual Control

In the highly developed form that analogue management reaches in many large companies, subordinates can actually use the control system to isolate themselves from their superiors. Managers can find themselves negotiating targets with their subordinates as if they were having a relationship with a vendor or customer instead of another member of the management team (and a subordinate at that!).

To the extent that the manager attempts to reassert his control, the subordinate may threaten to take less responsibility for the analogue results and thereby hold his superior at bay. Subordinates are often quite aggressive on this issue, especially if there is incentive compensation involved.

Analogue Management Can Discourage Good Managers from Acting in the Company's Interest

In the analogue management environment, the subordinate manager or nonmanager can be faced with a superior who is very interested in the analogue results and little else. As we have just seen, they may not even have a very good understanding of what the subordinate really does. Because the superior communicates that her or she is more interested in the sales quota or the production schedule than about why the subordinate is having trouble achieving the goal, the subordinate may stop looking for help and do whatever is expedient to please their supervisor. This can be anything from shipping faulty products to selling at a low margin or anything else that improves one or more of analogues without lowering any other of *his or her* analogues.

The insidious reality is that he or she has a negative incentive to make choices that are good for the company but bad for his or her performance as measured by his analogue. This type of situation not only damages the company's performance in the short run, but hurts the future as well since many of the choices, such as shipping faulty product, will have longer-term consequences.

Analogue Management Frequently Causes the Wrong Executives to be Promoted, Often all the Way to Top Management

The next to last thing a company needs is a group of managers who will routinely put their own short-run interest above that of the company. The last thing it needs is a system that rewards this kind of behavior above constructive company-oriented behavior. The sad fact is that in the highly developed form in which it is found in many American companies, analogue management does just that. It rewards the wrong people. American business abounds with managers who got where they are by "making their numbers" no matter what. It would be nice if we could say they were tough, insightful managers who also did those things that the analogues don't measure at the same time. In fact, this is frequently not the case, as witnessed by our obsolete product offerings and sliding market positions.

Analogue management has an additional and somewhat more subtle effect on the promotion process. Besides favoring self-oriented executives, it also favors the bureaucratic over the operating manager. It is no accident that accountants and lawyers have fared so well in large American companies since the 1950s. The management systems favor people with this background. Analogue management can easily be a system that favors self-oriented bureaucrats over company-oriented operating executives.

RELATIONSHIP TO AMERICA'S PROBLEM

The problems described in this chapter are many of the very problems that American managers and American companies are accused of having. *There is a cause behind the American management malaise and its name is analogue management.* Until we come to grips with this reality, there is no hope of improving our management process to the degree necessary to assure our competitive success in a world economy.

CHAPTER 4

THE MYTH OF "GROWTH" AS A MEASURE OF MANAGEMENT SUCCESS

Of all the havoc inflicted on the management of American companies by the analogue management process, the worst by far, in my view, has been the infatuation with corporate growth as measured by these analogues. Clearly a need exists to understand whether a business is improving, static, or declining as a competitive entity. This is the real test of the management's value-creation process. Any success or difficulty in the short run can be due to a number of factors beyond management's immediate control. However, over time they should succeed or be replaced.

In the analogue-focused American management system, we have chosen to obtain this longer view of a company's performance by measuring its growth defined as increases in sales, earnings, and/or assets.

In the last few years, when it has been popular to challenge our management system, this concept of growth (as measured by the accounting system) has escaped the barrage of criticism almost unscathed. People criticizing the focus on quarterly earnings seem to see nothing wrong in defining short-term (year to year) sales and earnings increases as positive proof of management success.

This fascination with growth as we measure it can be seen by the attention it gets in the business press. *Fortune Magazine* lists the:

- 500 Largest U.S. Industrial Corporations.
- Service 500—Largest U.S. Nonindustrial Corporations.
- 500 Largest International Corporations.

Each of these lists is published in separate issues and extensive analysis accompanies the lists showing things such as:

- Company movement within the list since the preceding year.
- Companies entering and leaving the list.
- Largest percentage gainers and losers.
- Changes within industry groups.

Fortune 500 has become an adjective, as in "That is a Fortune 500 company."

INC. Magazine has its 500 Fastest Growing Public Companies and 100 Fastest Growing Private Companies. Even specialized industry magazines have such lists. The American Banker has its "Top 100 U.S. Bank Holding Companies" (using assets) and Datamation publishes a list of the 100 largest companies in the data processing industry. When was the last time anyone defined getting higher up on one of these lists as being bad? Going down as being preferred? The lists themselves as irrelevant measures of *recent* corporate success?

Strategic analysis, that star of the 1970's management tool, also does not challenge growth as measured by the accounting system. The terms *Star, Dog and Cash Cow* are all synonymous with a company's present and expected rate of "growth." The growth they mean however, is almost always sales or earnings; the time frames are almost inevitably three to five years.

THIS APPROACH IS FUNDAMENTALLY FLAWED

Once again the chosen analogues cannot do what we ask of them. A company improves or declines competitively due to a number of factors including:

- Management action or inaction.
- Behavior of competitors.
- Changes in the environment.

Management and the other employees of the company carry on the competitive process as they do their daily jobs. Doing such things as:

- Conceiving competitive strategies.
- Developing product.
- Building the products or supplying the services.
- Contacting and selling to customers.
- Doing internal administrative work.

Progress in these areas, when taken together, determines if the company is "improving." Each area is, though, dimly visible to the accounting system. Further improvement, or lack of it, needs to be viewed in the context of changes in the business environment and the behavior of competitors. The accounting system is *blind* to these outside realities. *In spite of these difficulties, Americans have chosen a method of measuring corporate improvement that depends on the accounting system.*

Further, these measures are used as if the following two concepts are true:

- Growth, as measured by sales and profits, is such a good way to measure longer run corporate success that other measures are not needed. If a company is growing by these measures, it is improving. If it is static or declining, it is getting worse.
- Growth, as measured by this standard, must necessarily occur since it measures a company's improvement and companies must improve if they are to be regarded as well managed.

Growth in Sales and Earnings Is a Valid and Sufficient Way to Measure Corporate Improvement

Whether growth, as measured by the accounting system, is the proper way to judge a company's performance is essentially not challenged in our system; increasing sales and earnings means "better" and that's that. This blind faith, in turn, has led to some serious consequences including:

- The overvaluation of *short-run* changes in growth measurements.
- A focus on the *outcomes* as reported by the accounting measures versus an examination of the *reasons* for both long- and short-term changes in these measures.

Short-Run Changes Are Overvalued

As we saw in Chapter 2, the accounting system is not able to measure short-run profit very accurately because it does not recognize changes in the company's assets very well. Measuring just sales in the short run is a problem as well. Sales increases or decreases need to be viewed over several years to be useful indicators of a corporate success. Short run fluctuations can be caused by a number of factors such as shifts in the economy that are really beyond management's control.

The limited validity of growth as a measure of corporate improvement depends upon allowing the accounting results to "catch up" with the company's actual operations. Though we saw in Chapter 2 that this can never actually occur, one can at least argue that good accounting results over several years will generally reflect a successful performance. One could even argue that if over the same period sales and earnings increased significantly, the company experienced growth.

While it would be impossible to connect the actual time periods within which the good performance occurred with the time periods in which the accounting system reported them, ten good, consecutive years could make that consideration moot for all but the most recent three to four years. Most Americans, however, are only concerned with the most recent years, usually the last one or two. *We are focused on the very period where the conventional measures are the most misleading.*

The Tendency to Ignore the Causes of Growth

Since we are trained to accept the accounting system's reported results as being absolutely valid, there is a great reluctance to adjust the reported numbers for causes that may not signal true improvement, assuming for the moment that growth of sales or earnings overtime actually measures improvement. Two more obvious cases are growth by inflation and growth by acquisition.

Growth achieved primarily by inflation seems to be ignored. In fact, it is relatively easy to find references to record sales or earnings in the president's letter in the annual report when these "records" were purely the result of inflation.

Whatever happened to inflation-adjusted accounting? One would think that would be the one safe adjustment to make since the SEC now requires that this data be reported. Instead the SEC-required inflation-adjusted data appear back with the notes in corporate financial statements, rarely receiving a mention in the president's letter or anywhere else in the annual report. I believe that the "anti-growth" characteristics of inflation-adjusted accounting basically killed any interest in it. This occurred in spite of the fact that inflation-adjusted accounting had the tremendous potential to prevent paying taxes on inflated profits.

Likewise a major component of reported sales and earnings often comes from business units that have been acquired. "Growth" through acquisition is viewed as being equivalent to internally generated growth. While some note may be taken in the year of the acquisition, succeeding years' reports will make no effort to separate the two.

Growth as Measured Must Necessarily Occur if a Company Is Well Managed

Since we believe that growth as measured is monitoring corporate *improvement,* to be against growth is to be against getting better (clearly an untenable position for any manager). Since "getting better" does not have any obvious natural constraints, one does not often see or hear references to a "reasonable" rate of growth. In fact CEOs frequently make statements that talk about 15 percent growth rates and doubling the size of their company in five years not only as attainable but also as proper corporate growth objectives. When is the last time anyone heard a CEO say that his company cannot safely grow more than 2 percent above inflation? Or that the company cannot profitably employ its cash flow so it will pay out the surplus cash flow in dividends? Unfortunately this has become very difficult to do because of the naive way the American system treats growth as measured.

As the 1960s and 1970s wore on:

- We became increasingly focused on growth as a measure of corporate performance.
- We became increasingly less critical of the reasons behind the growth that we were seeing and the percentage increases that were being claimed.

The result was that many companies felt they could and should obtain what would have been unbelievable growth rates before this period. Indeed, managements tools were developed to help them to do this.

Two new management techniques were "invented" during this period: Formal Corporate Planning and Strategic Analysis. Formal (sometimes referred to as "Long-Range") Planning appeared first in the 1960s, followed by the Strategic Management concepts in the 1970s. Both were aimed at doing a better job of managing the corporation in time frames exceeding one year.

As with most "new" management techniques, both Corporate Planning and Strategic Management were codifications of existing management techniques. Once these techniques had names and formal definitions they evolved rapidly. The word spread through channels such as articles in the business press, and through technical societies, business school classes, and consultants.

However, both Corporate Planning and Strategic Management evolved after we had developed a management style that focused on managing analogued *results rather than activities*. American companies had already fallen into the analogue management trap. These techniques were merely a byproduct, yet *these tools played a major role in a scenario which saw our fascination with growth, as defined, become a major destroyer of American business vitality through encouraging manipulation of the corporate structure and other counter productive behavior.* It is worth discussing Corporate Planning and Strategic Management separately to demonstrate this point.

Corporate Planning

In its original conceptualization, corporate planning was intended to focus top management on the longer run issues. Corporations using this technique were usually careful to include other corporate "objectives" in the process in addition to growth in sales and earnings. Most companies had objectives for quality, employee relations, community responsibility, and so forth.

Having defined the corporation's objectives, the planning process goes on to define the strategies and tactics that will be used to attain these objectives. Usually these strategies are developed after an attempt is made to define the level of achievement the company can expect if it "does nothing" (i.e., what will happen, say, over the next five years, as a result of the corporation's current momentum). The gap between expected and desired levels of achievement is the "planning gap" that the new strategies are intended to eliminate. Because of the way growth was defined, efforts to attain the company's objectives by eliminating this formally determined planning gap led to some very wasteful behavior. Let's see how.

For two very good reasons, most larger companies are able to create five-year financial operating plans and little else. The two reasons are:

- The corporation is not set up to report nonfinancial analogues on a credible basis.
- Daily management controls are rooted in the financial system.

The credibility problem makes it difficult for an analogue manager to monitor activities, such as planned improvements to the distribution system, which do not produce reliable short run measurements of results. As a consequence, these activities tend to drift gradually out of the senior management process. Meanwhile, the lower level managers, who are actually doing the work of improving our hypothetical distribution system, must accomplish their task in the face of an unyielding, current year financial plan. Further achievement of the financial plan frequently affects their compensation.

As a result, the corporate plan gradually evolves into a longer-range financial plan. As one division president once told me during his company's annual five-year planning process, "I can change anything I want to in the five-year plan I submitted last year except the financial results and I will not be questioned by corporate. If I change the financial section even a little bit I will be challenged."

If growth of sales and earnings is defined as management progress, this is not a devastating problem. One can use a financial plan to manage increases in sales and earnings as long as one is not too critical about how this is being accomplished.

For example, a number of companies defined "growth" strategies to fill the planning gap that called for acquiring another company. Think of that—acquire a company to increase the reported sales and earnings. Is it any wonder that the logic used to justify some acquisitions is so poor when viewed in retrospect? Many other strategies were not well planned but focused on the "need" to meet the growth targets as defined. Analogue management had successfully extended its reach several years into the future by using a management technique that was intended to do just the opposite.

Strategic Analysis

Since in the 1970s growth was firmly established as a measure of corporate success, it was only a small step to a logical fallacy that said: "We can grow faster (and therefore be better regarded) if we own companies that already or will soon grow rapidly themselves." Best of all is to own good companies in fast-growing industries.

Companies had used acquisitions to improve reported results for years. ("Buying" earnings using their superior stock market price/earning ratio was a favorite technique of the conglomerates that appeared in the 1960s.) Corporate Planning created an acceptance of the notion that acquisitions could be used for improving reported growth within the relatively short (usually five-year) planning cycle. It didn't take much imagination to take the next step. The era of the "Dog," the "Star," and most importantly, the "Cash Cow" was born.

Strange Behavior Can Result

Pursuit of growth, as measured in our system, can explain some management behavior which could otherwise seem irrational. For example:

- Why did Bank of America, Continental Illinois, and the major New York banks all have troubled loans which threatened their solvency from different types of borrowers?
- Why did so many companies such as CBS systematically use the earnings of their very profitable core business to buy less profitable companies where they had little management expertise, rather than pay larger dividends to their stockholders?
- Why did Michael Porter, the author of the best book on corporate strategy,[1] find in a recent study[2] of 33 prestigious American companies that most had divested more acquisitions than they had retained?

These apparently irrational actions have resulted from the struggle to grow or to maintain size. The fact that this goal might not have been in the stockholders' interest (or, for that matter might be threatening to the corporations' very existence) seems to have been missed or, more likely, ignored.

As the large corporate customers of the money center banks found alternatives in the commercial paper and bond

---

[1]Michael E. Porter, *Competitive Strategy* (Free Press, 1980).

[2]Michael E. Porter, "From Competitive Advantage to Corporate Strategy," *Harvard Business Review* (May–June 1987), pp. 43–59.

markets, the volume of high quality loans available to the major banks declined. However, banks are measured by asset size and rather than let their assets "growth" cease, many large banks made increasingly risky loans. The most famous loans, of course, were to Third World countries. In the short run, the accounting system booked these high-risk loans as assets and, because it couldn't tell, ignored the increased risk. It is worth noting that it took much longer than the three-to-five year period we seem to focus on for the high risk of these loans to manifest itself.

CBS, and the companies in Michael Porter's study, as well as many other American companies over the last 20 to 30 years have used the same logic, but have substituted high-risk acquisitions for high-risk loans. Many of these companies were facing diminished rates of growth in their core business. Others simply wanted to grow faster than their internal capacity to do so. Some were so displeased with what they saw as the future of their core business, that they were anxious to leave it completely or at least get most of their earnings from some industry that seemed to have better growth prospects.

In general, these companies made no secret of their intentions regardless of their perceived growth "problem." Every acquisition based on their growth problem was reported with great interest in the business press. Business schools built cases around their "strategic" activity. Many of the best young people going into business wanted to be in the corporate planning area where these acquisitions were being studied and implemented.

When the restructuring corporate raiders first appeared on the scene, they were scorned as financial manipulators who could never manage the targeted companies. The newly invented junk bonds were pointed to as making it possible for these men to do their dirty work. Over the last few years, no matter what one thinks of raiders, it has become very clear that many large corporations, when viewed from a stockholder's perspective, were very bad asset packages; much worse than most knowledgeable people would have believed they could be. Whether stockholder value can be significantly increased by raiders who may or may not be able to manage these companies successfully in the longer run is another issue. (In fact there has not been enough time to judge this.) What is clear, however, is one of the main reasons why they are getting a chance—misguided attempts to "grow" the business as we measure growth rather than as the economy does.

Once more analogue management has made its contribution to the competitiveness of American industry, this time not only by diverting management from managing the real business, but also by encouraging questionable behavior including manipulation of the corporate structure. After all, these activities produce growth, and growth means the company is being well managed.

CHAPTER 5

THE COMMONLY USED ANALOGUES ARE TECHNICALLY FLAWED

Up to now we have discussed the use of analogues in the management process in terms of their limitations in being what we want them to be and our overreliance on them in this context. Throughout this discussion there has been an unspoken assumption that the analogues are at least technically correct within their limitations. That is, a product cost or a profitability measurement, for example, is correct within the limitations of the accounting system to make these measurements. In this chapter we will deal with the issue of technical correctness. In doing so, the fundamental thesis will be that analogues are *not* technically correct.

In order to make this point as simply and emphatically as possible, comment will be limited to those analogues that are commonly produced by publicly held companies using internally generated financial data. This approach is used for the following reasons:

- Because of FASB rules, SEC regulations, and the demands of outside auditors and financial analysts, accounting data in publicly held companies are the most "standards-driven" data in common use in American business.
- The techniques used to produce these analogues are well understood. Therefore, there is a considerable

degree of uniformity in the ways various companies prepare them.
- The techniques are also well understood by outsiders, who also use them for their own purposes such as lending or investing.

Clearly, if these analogues are technically wrong, a great deal of damage is being done. In addition, if these well-understood and widely used computations are wrong, it says a great deal about the technical veracity of analogues that are less widely used and come from less tightly controlled data.

Basically the modern American company uses accounting data in its internal management process in two ways:

- To better understand the business.
- To better control day-to-day operations.

In the first case, the accounting system is used to *measure* certain characteristics of the business. These measurements include the following analogues:

- The cost of producing a product or service (so-called "cost accounting").
- The profitability of a product or product line; a customer; or a geographic area.
- The return on a proposed investment.

In the second case, when management is attempting to use accounting data to better control day-to-day operations, cost and revenue data is reported against preset targets by the responsible executive. Examples would include reports such as these:

- Profitability against a profit plan.
- Expense against budgets.
- Revenue against quotas.

The techniques for using accounting data to develop these sorts of analogue measures of the business are well understood and generally taught in business schools. As a result, there is a great deal of similarity in the way that "well-managed" companies make these calculations in practice.

It is also true, however, that the usual ways in which these calculations are done are technically wrong; improbable as this may seem given their widespread use. They are wrong because of mistakes we make in both the measurement and control calculations themselves. *They are also wrong because we sometimes confuse measurement and control and try to do them both at the same time. This, it turns out, is technically impossible.*

How these errors are made will be illustrated by taking an example from the measurement side, product costing, and one from the control side, departmental budgeting. These examples have been chosen because in each case the overwhelming majority of companies use versions of the same approach for handling them. Subsequently, how we make technical mistakes in both the measurement and control areas by confusing the two will be shown.

ERRONEOUS PRODUCT COSTING

For simplicity let's use the costing of manufactured products in this example. In fact, the same product-costing techniques are used in service industries such as hospitals, insurance companies, and banks to determine the cost of their service products (and therefore they make the same mistakes).

Basically the technique used for costing a product is to "apply" all factory costs, but no other company costs, to the various products that are produced. Factory costs naturally divide into the following three major categories:

- Direct material.
- Direct labor.
- Factory overhead (i.e., all other factory costs).

There are a number of acceptable techniques for applying these costs to the various products produced in the factory such as actual cost, average cost, and standard cost. The standard cost method is by far the most frequently used in sophisticated American companies. It is intended to be the normal cost of the product under normal conditions and is usually expressed as:

Direct material	$X
Direct labor	$Y
Overhead	$Z
Total cost per unit of measure =	$X + $Y + $Z

Direct material is the material actually used in the product including normal scrap of this material. (All other plant materials such as grease are in overhead.) Direct labor is the labor actually used in fabricating and assembling the product. (Material handling for example is in overhead.) Overhead is all factory costs that are not direct material and direct labor.

The trick is to assign all these costs to the various plant-created products. Direct material and direct labor are relatively easy. Using industrial engineering techniques the amount of "normal" direct material and direct labor can be determined and entered onto the product cost sheet (or computer record).

The essential problem is determining how much overhead to assign to the various products. In almost all modern American factories, overhead is also the single largest category of product cost—usually 50 percent or more of the total. It would not be unusual for the three types of costs to break down as follows:

	Percentage of Product Cost
Direct Material	30–40%
Direct Labor	10–20%
Overhead	40–60%

Plant departments naturally divide into direct departments and indirect departments. Both types of departments incur overhead expenses that must be assigned to products. Direct departments are the departments that perform work directly on the product. They have names such as Stamping, Plating and Assembly. All other departments are indirect i.e., overhead departments, and include names such as Material Handling, Tool Room, and Plant Maintenance. The direct departments, by definition, incur all the direct materials and direct labor costs. However, they also have a number of overhead costs that must also be assigned to the products (often 10 to 20 different kinds). These are items of cost such as the foreman's salary, small tools, lubricants, and so forth. *All the expenses of the indirect departments are automatically categorized as overhead.*

The usual approach is to forecast what the production for the plant will be in the upcoming year. This production forecast is then converted into two elements needed to make the calculation:

- The amount of overhead expense that will be required in each of the *direct and indirect* departments for the year.
- The number of direct labor hours that will be needed for the year in each direct department to accomplish the forecasted production.

The cost accountants then determine an overhead rate per direct labor hour for each of the direct departments using the following approach:

- The accountants assign all of the forecasted indirect department expenses to the direct departments. The basis of this allocation is usually an estimate of the percentage of the services of an indirect department that is used by each direct department (for example, a press department presumably uses more of the services of a Tool Room than an assembly department does, etc.) (See Figure 5-1).
- The overhead expenses allocated to each direct department are then added to the overhead expenses of the direct departments themselves.
- The forecasted direct labor hours for each direct department are then divided into the total of the overhead

expense to create an overhead rate per direct labor hour for each direct department.

- Overhead is then assigned to products based on the direct labor hours each product uses in each direct department, multiplied by each department's overhead rate (see Figure 5-2).

This, in simplified form, is the so-called "full-absorption" product cost system sanctioned by FASB and the IRS and used by most American companies. As the volume of direct labor hours varies from the forecast throughout the year or the amount of overhead to be "absorbed" changes from the budgeted amounts, no changes are made to the product costs. In most companies these changes would be made at most annually.

The full-absorption cost system is also used to put product into finished-good inventory and remove it when it is sold as "cost of goods sold." The amount of overhead actually spent during a reporting period is compared to the amount transferred to inventory by the overhead rates of the goods produced during that period. To the extent that actual overhead is over- or under-absorbed it is treated as a current period item.

What is wrong with this "mainline" approach to product costing? *What is wrong is that this approach is absolutely inappropriate for use in daily management decision-making.*

FIGURE 5-1

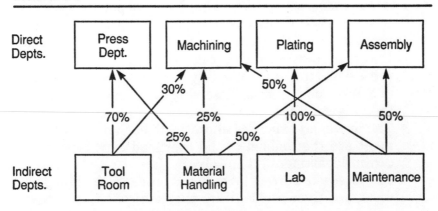

FIGURE 5-2

Dir. Labor Rate	8.00	9.00	11.00	5.00
Overhead Rates per DLH	15.00/DLH	12.00/DLH	18.00/DLH	8.00/DLH

Product A

Departmental Direct Labor Hours per 100 Units → | Press Dept. .5 DLH | → | Machining 1.0 DLH | → | Plating .2 DLH | → | Assembly 2.0 DLH |

Dir. Labor Cost	.5 × 8 = $4.00	1.0 × 9 = $9.00	.2 × 11 = $2.20	2.0 × 5 = $10.00
Overhead Cost	.5 × 15 = $7.50	1.0 × 12 = $12.00	.2 × 18 = $3.60	2.0 × 8 = $16.00

Product cost for Product A

Direct labor	4.00 + 9.00 + 2.20 + 10.00 =	$25.20
Direct material		30.00
Overhead	7.50 + 12.00 + 3.60 + 16.00 =	39.10
		$94.30/100 units

Product costs are used in making decisions such as whether to make or buy, in pricing, or in understanding issues such as product line, customer, or location profitability.

In computing product costs by these methods, overhead costs are treated as if they vary proportionally with direct labor hours. In fact this is not the case. A high percentage of overhead costs do not vary as the volume of production changes in the normal operating range of the plant. These are costs such as management, security, and depreciation. In addition, the balance of overhead costs have a large fixed component that maintains the minimum level of production (just like "fixed" costs) and creeps upward in irregular patterns as production increases. Between the two types, this "fixed" cost is normally 75 percent or more of all overhead cost. (And therefore 30 to 50 percent of product cost as computed!)

Fixed cost does not "go away" if the product is discontinued. It is not really a cost of making the product at all. How can it be? We are confusing these enterprise costs which are useful to the product,[1] with the idea that they are a cost of producing it. Products contribute margin to cover these costs.[2] Product costs can never be more than the incremental costs that are incurred because the product is produced. Therefore they can never be more than the following:

- The cost of direct material.
- The cost of direct labor.
- The amount that overhead actually increases because the product is manufactured and adds to plant volume.

In a make-or-buy decision the company will actually incur an outside expense to buy the product. Shouldn't this be matched against the inside expense that will actually be saved? *When product costs contain costs that won't be saved, we bias the system toward outside production* and the company toward less profitability.

Likewise, in trying to understand profitability, we need to know the "difference" between having and not having the volume associated with the product line or customer. This means we must be able to know the *incremental* cost versus the *incremental* volume. Our current product cost makes the products and customer seem significantly less profitable than they actually are, causing us to treat them accordingly, often with disastrous results as the volume disappears and 30–50 percent of the cost doesn't.

Many defenders of the full-absorption system point to pricing decisions to support their position. They point out the need to cover "all" the company's costs not just the incremental costs of producing more product. This thinking overlooks the fact that prices are set in the markektplace. A company that can see the effect of extra volume on its costs, and therefore the

---

[1]If usefulness to the product is the proper criterion, why not include nonfactory overhead such as sales, engineering, and accounting?

[2]Whatever happened to marginal cost versus marginal revenue from our beginning economics courses?

profitability of that volume, is better off than one that can't. Full-absorption costing says incremental sales produce more fixed costs. They do not, as the Japanese have taught us! If knowing the incremental profitability of products creates pricing "difficulty," the company has another problem and full-absorption cost accounting is not the way to fix it.

Product modification does not benefit from full-absorption costing. In fact, the only way to affect a product's true cost to the company is to modify its material or direct labor costs. Reductions in overhead expense (even variable overhead) benefit all products.

The plain fact is that because they include a large percentage of "fixed costs" the overwhelming percentage of American product costs are wrong and they are wrong high! This causes companies to:

- Undervalue product.
- Undervalue customers.
- Overprice.

Cost overstatement, which understates true margin, leads to an unwillingness to invest in products and customers and therefore causes difficulty in attaining the scale necessary to produce efficiency. It is worth noting that these are some of the very problems American managers are accused of not handling well.

Interestingly it doesn't look like American companies are about to change. Most of the current criticism of the product costing system, to the extent there is any, seems to center on the use of direct labor hours as a means for moving overhead to the products. These critics point out that when current full-absorbtion techniques for product costing were developed decades ago, the percentage of product cost that was direct labor was double current levels. Overhead has since grown and direct labor has decreased as mechanization has been substituted for labor. Therefore, they seem to be saying, what is needed is a more precise method of assigning this increasingly important overhead cost to products. While this discussion is well beyond the scope of this chapter, it is worth noting that this could result in applying more "fix" cost to products that will not "go away" if the products do.

ERRONEOUS DEPARTMENTAL BUDGET REPORTS

Perhaps the most ubiquitous control analogue used in American business is the expense budget. In previous chapters we have dealt with its limitations as an analogue of management performance. Let's focus on the budgeting approach used by American companies from a *technical* perspective.

As with product costing, there is a great deal of similarity in the approach companies, especially large ones, use to control their expenses. Most knowledgeable people would agree that the technical objective of expense-control reporting is to report actual spending against preassigned targets in as unambiguous and technically defensible a manner as possible. This is particularly important because in our management system we take this particular control analogue quite seriously.

As in the case of cost accounting the desired result is frequently not achieved. Because it is not, what should be a relatively straightforward management process often turns into a process fraught with acrimony and negative behavior as managers either feel manipulated by the system or are themselves trying to manipulate it. Our rather "hard-nosed" style of requiring managers to meet their expense targets only exacerbates the problem.

To understand how we do this rather ordinary process poorly from a technical point of view, let us start with describing the approach used by most companies. To accomplish control, companies create cost centers. These cost centers can be direct or indirect departments in a factory, sales offices, or an accounting function. The only requirement is that the cost center report to a single responsible executive. The cost centers can be aggregated up the organization chart, making it possible to have cost-control responsibility starting at first-level supervision or at any level above according to the desires of the executives involved.

Each of the budget entities has a number of expense accounts within which the costs incurred by that department are accumulated. Each of these accounts will also have a budget. Reports are prepared, usually monthly, that compare actual expenditures against these budgets account by account. Variances, both positive and negative, are computed for each account and for the cost center as a whole. Control is achieved by requiring the responsible executive to explain his variances. This requirement is intended to accomplish the following purposes:

- To give the responsible executive the information and presumably the incentive to manage his expenditures to the agreed-upon target.
- To give higher level executives the information they need to supervise the various cost centers for which they are responsible.
- To provide the management team with a way of communicating about cost-control problems. By using the budget-variance explanation process they can effect needed changes in spending behavior.

For real control to occur a situation must be achieved where every expenditure in the control system meets three criteria:

- That it be assignable to a single cost-control center which has a single executive responsible for explaining variances.
- That it be "under the control" of that cost-control center executive.
- That it be reported against a "fair" (previously agreed-upon) target.

If all three conditions are met, it would seem reasonable to hold the executives in control of each of the budget-reporting (cost-control) centers, responsible for explaining any budget variances. *These three conditions are rarely met in the budgeting systems of American companies.*

The most flagrant problems exist in the areas of charging expenses to the wrong cost centers and having goals for individual accounts that are not technically correct. In this example we will focus on the problem of charging expenses to the proper cost center. According to the second of our three criteria, expense must be charged to the cost-center manager who controls it. But what defines control? Who controls a given expenditure, the executive who made it or the executive who benefits from it?

Viewing the way many American companies handle this problem, one would think it was one of life's (or at least business') great mysteries. The majority of companies go in both directions. They charge most expenses to the department that incurs them, but allocate some expenses from "spending" departments to "using" departments. When one attempts to determine how the company chooses one or the other approach, there is rarely any general rule to be found.

However if one looks closely over several companies, there seems to be an underlying assumption. The assumption is that "the less the spender of a particular expense uses or 'benefits' from that expense himself the more likely it is to be allocated." One is more likely to see heat, light, and power allocated in the factory, and data processing in the office, since the plant engineer uses little power and presumably the data processing department does little work for itself.

The usual reason given for allocating from spenders to users, is that the only way the spender can "control" the expense is to "incentivise" the user with a cross-charge, so he will not overuse data processing services or whatever else is being allocated to him. On the surface at least, allocating these types of expenses would seem to make sense. But where do we draw the line between those expenses that we control through incentivising users and those we leave with the spending organization?

In a modern business organization, almost all the work in the organization is done to benefit some other part of the company. While the indirect departments in the factory are an obvious example, this is even more true when one looks at the "white-collar" departments. The credit department supports sales. The accounting department supports almost every other department (with budget reports if nothing else!). Personnel may support both blue-collar and white-collar departments, and so forth.

What keeps all these users from abusing the organizations that support them and thereby causing these organizations to exceed their budgets? Why don't we allocate all the costs to all the users? (In some large companies the only reason we don't seems to be the resistance of the "using" department combined with the sheer technical and physical problem of getting it done!)

In a division of a large publicly held company, there were about 1,000 cross-charges per month. About half were "permanent." The departments involved agreed to the routine monthly cross-charges. However, because the practice was acceptable, the other half of the charges occurred spontaneously. Costs were transformed from spending cost centers to "users" of that department's service because the spending department believed something unusual had occurred and they, the doing department, should not have to pay for it.

In fact, in spite of its widespread use in American business, *the idea that costs can be better controlled by allocating them to users is technically fallacious*. There are two simple reasons for this fact; either one of which would be sufficient to invalidate the methodology as a control tool:

- The using departments are unable to explain their variances.
- There are no allocation methods that are technically defensible.

When a cost-center manager is asked to explain a variance in an allocated expense account, say data processing expense, he will usually say something like "I don't understand this variance. I asked the data processing department how much to budget each month and that's the amount I put in my budget. I don't know why the charge this month is higher than that." Factory departments will have similar responses.

If the spending department—for example, our data processing department—attempts to defend the charge based on increased usage, an argument over the allocation method is likely to develop. This disagreement with the allocation method will probably occur whether or not the method of allocation has been agreed upon before the year began. This is because there are no really good ways to handle many of the following technical problems of allocation:

- Fixed versus variable costs.
- Fixing costs to the transactions that actually caused them.
- User versus producer blame for a cost increase.

Fortunately, a company can achieve its budgetary control objective quite nicely without allocating any expenses. The two objectives of control for executives charged with an expense *are met in all cases by assigning the expense to the executive who spends the money.* In effect, the spending executive is responsible for both doing a good job of using his budget and of controlling the use of his services.

In our example, the plant engineer and the data processing manager really are making the decisions that result in the way their services are supplied. Why then shouldn't they be responsible for their budget performance? But what about user abuse? When they put their budgets together, of necessity both of these executives made assumptions about user needs. If these assumptions were wrong, or if the users' behavior changed, who is in a better position to explain the variances that are created than the individual who created the budgets? This budgeting approach must work. It is the way the overwhelming majority of all the expense dollars are controlled, even in the companies that allocate costs.

CONFUSING MEASUREMENT AND CONTROL

Another major source of technical problems in American management analogues is confusing measurement and control reporting. These are two distinct functions created for two different purposes.

Measurements are intended to help management better understand the business and react tactically or even strategically. A company needs to be informed about the cost of a product or the profitability of a retail branch store in order to make product or location decisions, not to control its day-to-day revenue and expense. The revenue and expense control occurs in the control system against targets by the responsible executives.

However, managements *like* to be able to control against measurements as well. Why not control against product cost or customer profitability? In many ways these seem like more meaningful targets than revenue by territory or expense by spending department.

These issues can be managed. What we *can't* do is create a technically sound *control report* which makes these results the responsibility of a *single* executive for two very simple reasons:

- Companies are not organized this way. Companies are organized functionally—products and customers, and almost anything else the company measures for tactical reasons, are not the responsibility of a single executive. Therefore, at least two of the conditions needed for a control report to be technically sound—a single responsible executive—in control of the costs and revenues for which he or she is responsible—are missing.
- Transfer pricing and cost allocation do not work well enough to be used for control purposes.

Our analogue-driven approach to management finds this unacceptable so control reports are manufactured anyway. This situation is particularly true of large service companies such as banks. These control reports are monuments to allocation. The revenue and the overwhelming percentage of the cost in a bank's customer profitability report, as received by the responsible executive, come from the activities of organizations outside of his or her management control.

While assigning executives customer responsibility may be logical, acting as if they really have control of revenues and expenses does not make a great deal of sense. Reports reflecting this position give the executive more incentive to "work" the details of the reporting system's revenue-recognition and transfers-pricing procedures than to actually work on the bank's relationship with the customers for whom he is responsible. We have all seen such counterproductive behavior and usually deplore it. However, when we see it from the perspective of an executive trapped under a reporting system that he feels is technically arbitrary, what can we expect?

This reporting system demonstrates the same bias toward analogues that we have been discussing. Management of an activity has been equated to holding a single executive responsible for its outcome, *whether this is technically possible or not*; and responsibility has come to mean responsibility vis-a-vis an analogued target. All other management alternatives are virtually ignored.

Additionally, as we saw with product costing, a number of the costs involved in serving a bank customer, like executive time and computer equipment leases or depreciation, are fixed. They are, insensitive to volume changes in the normal operating range. Spreading these fixed costs to customers has the same effect—distorting the true cost of serving them. Therefore, this approach not only mixes up control and measurement but can also become the source of an erroneous measurement of the cost of servicing the customer.

SUMMARY

This chapter is intended to illustrate another problem with our analogue management system that seems to get little attention, technical problems with the analogues themselves.

The problems mentioned are merely a few illustrations of a widespread problem in this area.

In my view, the reason that these problems do not get more attention, even in the business schools, is that we *want* so badly to have analogues that work that we are psychologically biased against critical examination of them. The first several chapters have focused on our penchant to ignore the inherent limitations of analogues as management tools. This chapter demonstrates that this tendency even extends to their technical soundness.

PART 2

ESCAPING THE ANALOGUE TRAP

INTRODUCTION

The purpose of Part I of this book was to explain why American companies seem unable to improve the American management process in the face of our manifest dissatisfaction with the results it produces. It points out that the process I call analogue management not only inherently produces the problems facing American managers, but also contains within itself the seeds of its own perpetuation.

The first chapter points out that the American management process is caught in an analogue management trap. By doing the following we are overemphasizing analogues:

- Believing they are more comprehensive and more accurate than they really are.
- Believing that we can control against analogues and, thereby, effectively manage the underlying business activities.
- Not understanding that managing against analogues is self-fulfilling.

Chapter 2 attempts to show that the central analogue used in American business—the accounting system—is severely flawed; in fact, that it is essentially useless as a measurement of the performance of a company in the time spans (a month, a quarter, a year) within which we are using it.

Chapter 3 points out that our reliance on analogue management has led to many problems, such as the following:

- Believing top management can have more control over short-run operations than it really can.
- Biasing the value-creation process away from off-balance-sheet corporate assets such as market position.
- Hindering the ability of individual departments and even divisions to cooperate with each other.
- Making American corporations less nimble than they would otherwise be.
- Making American corporations more inward-looking.
- Creating incentive-compensation systems that are naive and often counterproductive.
- Putting negative pressures on individual executives as they attempt to operate in the company's best interest.

Chapter 4 points out that our fascination with analogue measures has caused us to define a corporation's improvement over time as "getting bigger" as measured by accounting measures such as sales and total profits. This has, in turn, led to a great deal of counterintuitive management behavior that has resulted in the waste of large amounts of corporate resources.

Chapter 5 points out that our fascination with managing using analogues has caused us to make a number of very basic errors in the internal reports that are used by most corporations. Further, that despite the problems these errors cause in the management decision-making process, they are almost never discussed by the business intellectual community.

Clearly nothing would stop managers who are convinced by the arguments in the first part of this book from modifying their behavior as they see fit under the circumstances. One could even argue that this would be a good place to end this book.

However, it may be easier to exit the analogue management trap than to know what to do when one is out. As suggested in Chapter 1, analogue management is the only system we know and many senior managers are where they are because they are good at using it. Furthermore, it is the basis of most of what one reads in the business press and what is taught in our business schools. The next seven chapters deal with this problem. One has to ask how best to approach it. In one sense "what to do instead" could conceivably encompass the whole of the management process.

The approach I have chosen, tries to offer a number of suggestions that can be tried individually or in almost any combinations. As a practicing management consultant, I have tried to make suggestions that can be practically implemented by managers who have been successful in the current management system. All of the suggestions involve areas of some personal experience and are intended to augment the quality with which the "real" business activities are managed.

The chapters are arranged in a sequence that takes the reader conceptually farther and farther away from the current management techniques. However, none of the suggestions require a company to abandon any of its current reporting or management practices, although clearly changes in both are recommended.

Part II begins with Chapter 6—Using Analogues in a More Insightful Fashion. This chapter points out that management's concentration on controlling to the monthly financial plan has a triple-barreled negative effect. First, the information needed to run the real business is in short supply. Secondly, we refuse to use data that could be helpful and is already available. Finally, we believe that vigorous financial management produces better financial results than it actually does. The chapter describes why this happens, and suggests ways in which a significant amount of useful data on the real business can be created. If this sounds like a plan for more analogues, it is. However, the reader will see a principle that, when understood, will produce a material improvement in the information about real business operations over and above that whichthe overwhelming majority of companies now receive.

Chapter 7—Getting the Management Reports Right—deals with methods to make management reports right technically, whether management is using accounting or nonaccounting data or a combination of the two. It draws a distinction between reports used for controlling and those used for measuring the various aspects of the business and describes some principles that must be followed if these reports are to be correct. Solutions to the technical problems described in Chapter 5 are presented.

Chapter 8—Better Managing the Company's Largest Single Cost—Overhead—points out that, while overhead is by far the largest expense category in almost all American companies, it is seriously undermanaged in our present system. The only real control most companies have is over how much will be spent in a time period. They have almost no idea of what these expenditures are for or how they support the company's basic competitive activities. Suggestions are made that would help a company to understand and better manage overhead in terms of what it does for the company rather than who spends it in what time period. Since most of the "investments" in the company's off-balance-sheet assets are made through these accounts this is particularly important.

Chapter 9—Seizing the Opportunity to Better Manage Service—focuses on improving the service in which the company *wraps* its various products, whether the company is a manufacturing or a service company. Ways are suggested in which this process can be better managed by first understanding the three fundamental laws that make supplying service a continuing competitive opportunity:

- Service cannot be inventoried; it must be supplied on demand.
- Service is experienced by individual human beings each in his or her own terms.
- Service can take the form of a bewildering number of transactions planning for which can be very difficult.

Methods are suggested for supplying service which do not attempt to repeal these "laws."

By far the most comprehensive in its suggestions for managing the real business, Chapter 10—Continuous Competitive Advantage—demonstrates that most of what passes for corporate strategy today is not only useless but actually can be and has been dangerous. The chapter defines the role that strategy can play, defines the role of the core business unit competitively and suggests that the basis of competition is ultimately an organizational issue. In this context, a concept is introduced that I choose to call "continuous competitive advantage."

Chapter 11—Core Competitive Policies and Horizontal Management—builds on the concepts put forward in Chapter 10. It tries to answer this question: If the basis of competition is organizational, are there fundamental management principles that can be used to improve a company's chance of winning this competition?

Two principles are advocated. One, "Core Policies," postulates that most of what a company's human organization is, or ever will be, is a function of day in and day out management policies. That is, it is impossible to separate the development of the company's organizational strength and the way that the company deploys that organization in the daily competitive battle.

The second principle is the need to manage the company horizontally across the various functional organizations as well as vertically down them. The chapter points out that, while the customer only buys the product of this horizontal organization it, (the horizontal organization) is rarely consciously managed in our system. (This is another consequence of analogue management which, as we practice it, only works down the organization structure). Examples of how to make use of both these principals in the daily management process are described.

Chapter 12—Thoughts on Implementation—deals with the issue of implementation as a management process that can be thought of as independent of what is being implemented. Some suggestions about this process are offered in the context of implementing some of the ideas in this book.

Obviously, these chapters are not a complete selection of all the management ideas a manager fresh from the analogue management trap can use. Hopefully, they will be useful in some combination to most readers. The key is that none of these approaches requires a manager or a company to convince *anyone* that the analogue management trap even exists, or to make wholesale modifications in the company's reporting or other management systems to begin to get benefits from these ideas.

While the analogue management system deserves to be modified in some very fundamental ways, it is important that this modification take place in a way that does not create a discontinuity during which there is no management process at all.

CHAPTER 6

USING ANALOGUES IN A MORE INSIGHTFUL FASHION

What then is the role of analogues in the modern American management process? To begin with, it is not wrong to want analogue representations of business operations. They have existed since human beings have been able to write. Double-entry bookkeeping goes back centuries. Operational measures, such as cost per ton of output for textile mills, or cost per ton-mile for railroads, or inventory turnovers for retailers, were being used in the 19th century. It is not irrational to want to measure "growth" where growth is defined to mean how much progress a business is making in improving its competitive position over time. It is also much safer to use analogues once their limitations are understood. In fact, because of the way we have come to use analogues, *the modern manager is dangerously short of valid analogue measures that he knows how to use properly.*

In the overwhelming majority of companies, the dominant short-run measure is performance against the monthly financial plan. Because accounting data are regarded as more valid than other analogues, management, *particularly top management,* tends to *undervalue those measurements that cannot be "added" into the accounting system.* For example, because they cannot be expressed in terms of dollars, measures such as performance against shipment dates promised to customers may exist in the company but rarely make it into the monthly "package" reviewed by senior management. Yet, as we have seen, the accounting system is almost incapable of analoguing the performance of a business in the short run. Small changes in sales or fixed cost cause profits to jump all over the place.

As a result, management is not getting much help from the analogues it is using. *Because it is not focused on developing and using other analogues, both financial and nonfinancial, it is starved for the information it needs to manage the real activities of the business and to monitor progress over time.*

It is quite possible to develop, or begin to use a number of analogue measures which are:

- More valid.
- More accurate.
- More objective.
- Just as auditable.

These analogues can be used for both measurement and control activities and per se do not require that any analogues that management is currently using be abandoned.

HOW TO CREATE ANALOGUES AND USE THEM PROPERLY

In order to deal with the proper use of analogues in the business management process, it is necessary to deal with the fundamental logical error delaying progress in this area: the notion that the value of a measure depends on its ability to relate to data that is produced by the accounting system. Most managers follow this approach for at least three reasons:

- The accounting system seems to integrate the various pluses and minuses of the business and summarize them into a single "bottom-line" result.
- The accounting data, with its SEC regulations, Generally Accepted Accounting Principles, and outside auditing of results, seems more objective.
- Accounting data is acceptable to outsiders.

Making the results "addable" to the accounting system requires that all measurements be convertible to dollars. As we saw in Chapter 2, this need for a financial transaction is the very reason the accounting system is such a bad measurement device to begin with. The fact is, God (or Mother Nature if you prefer) did not create a reality within which business activity smoothly converts into financial transactions, however convenient that may have been! *It is not in our interest to ignore this reality.*

However, if progress is to be made, we not only have to understand the limitations of the accounting system and why measures that cannot be included in it are "all right" and probably even better; *it is also important to understand that there is no "other accounting system."* That is, nonaccounting measures are not only not addable to the accounting system, they cannot be added to each other to form a single comprehensive measure of success either. I seriously doubt if this will ever be possible. It is critical to understand this because our desire to have an overreaching analogue that sums up everything can be shifted from the accounting systems to some other wild measurement scheme if we are not careful.

Once we understand this principle, management is free to develop an almost limitless set of analogues that can be valuable in managing the business. However, they must be integrated using management's judgment. Again, except for the fact that we would prefer it to be different, there is nothing surprising about this. The world is full of examples where measures of the various aspects of a situation are integrated in the minds of people and meaningful action is taken. In the real world of business, this is the normal course of events.

The fact that management has to "judgmentally" integrate the various measures it may be trying to use to improve its insight into the business is not bad. *It is normal.* What is not normal is to pretend that the accounting system accurately integrates business results. Furthermore, realizing this need to integrate judgmentally leaves room in the decision process for the other information the manager needs which is not contained in any of the analogue outputs. Judgmental integrating of analogued and judgmental data is done all the time in the day-to-day management process.

Consider the decision to call on a customer. The salesman or sales manager integrates in his head some very complex probabilities associated with a number of short- and longer-range objectives. If given more data, such as the profit contribution of each product, a salesperson would be able to focus his or her efforts more intelligently. The essential rule for using measures to assist in managing the enterprise should be "do they improve the vision of reality enough to justify the expense of creating, maintaining, and using them?"

If managers do not insist on addability to the accounting system, they can create a number of perfectly objective and, if necessary, auditable measures that can be useful to management as it attempts to improve (grow) the business. For example, the following overall measures of the company's performance:

- Measures of product value to the customer such as defects in the first year of use, value of product features versus those of competitors at the same price point, and warranty expense per dollar of sales.
- Overall productivity such as sales per employee, an inflation-adjusted product cost index, and overhead per dollar of sales.
- Customer service indicies such as periodic customer service satisfaction surveys collecting comparable data, usage of a service guarantee if one exists, and various complaint and adjustment measures.
- Innovation indicies such as percentage of sales from new products and the position on the life cycle curve of the company's various products and services.
- Competitors' data indexed against company data and plotted historically by competitor to identify industry winners and losers.

Additionally, there is an almost unlimited opportunity to create analogues to help management better understand

and manage the more detailed aspects of the business, including:

- Time required to process various types of customer orders.
- Time required to process customer complaints.
- Errors per 1,000 invoices.
- Engineering releases per engineer.
- Employee turnover in various parts of the business.
- Tenure of college graduates who leave.

Clearly, the opportunity to use both "macro- and micro-analogues" is only limited by management's imagination and energy. These measures can be more "real" and, therefore, lead to more direct management action than the more abstract measures, such as the monthly profit.

Creating measures of your business that can be used to focus internal management activity and measure the results of this activity is also a low-risk effort for a number of reasons:

- The "capital investment" required to create these measures is low and the return is fast. In fact, such an effort should produce enough benefit by focusing management on the business realities to justify the effort involved almost immediately.
- The measures need not be perfect to be useful. Just as in the example of the salesperson, any additional information is potentially useful. It is not necessary to create a complete set of measures agreeable to all to experience the initial benefits.
- The measurements themselves and management's use of them will improve with time. The very act of trying to use the new measures will provide insights that will change the measurement themselves and the methodology used to make them. At the same time, management will be learning how to benefit from these new measures.
- Trying to create improved nonfinancial measures has an almost negligible downside. Less success probably means less benefit, not more trouble. Remember, the alternative is to believe the accounting system!

FINANCIAL PERFORMANCE IS STILL AN ISSUE

A number of readers, no matter how convinced of the inadequacies of the accounting system, may still regard these
concepts as fairly "avant-garde." How do we know, for example, that focusing on other measurements will not destroy a
company's financial performance as reported by the accounting system?

*The important thing to understand is that knowledge
does not force one to do anything.* As suggested above, the
traditional accounting controls do not disappear as one
focuses on more realistic measures. One still has as much
ability as ever to manage one's decisions in terms of their
potential accounting consequences.

What frightens some people when they contemplate running the business in a "less financially oriented" way is that
this approach will lead to making more investments in
"off-balance-sheet" assets. Since these investments will be
recorded as expenses in the current-period income statements, managers fear that profits will be destroyed. They
would contend that, since the investors and lender communi-
ties do not or will not understand this behavior, the corporation will be "punished" with lower stock prices, bond ratings,
and even loss of control of the company. Therefore, the
reasoning goes, their hands are tied. They are caught in the
analogue management trap and they cannot do anything
about it.

Many of the examples used to justify this argument
revolve around situations where earnings have been poor for
some time and management's explanation of how investments
are being made that the accounting system cannot "see" are
very vague. This vagueness stems from the very issues we are
discussing:

- Management offers little evidence to support its case
  that longer-run activities in which it claims to be
  investing will in fact improve the company's performance.

- Management doesn't explain in any *detail* the impact on reported financial results.

When a company actually develops new products or markets, and seriously tracks this activity, it can explain the impact on current earnings with some precision. Further, it can offer more convincing evidence of its progress in these specific areas.

DETAILED FINANCIAL MANAGEMENT IS NOT THE ANSWER

However, the real problem with this reasoning is focused in the assumption that short-run financial management is a viable alternative. Many managers believe it will produce better results, as reported by the financial system, than managing for the long run. This is not true, even in the relatively short term. Let's see why.

A company earning a reasonable return already has viable quantities of the on-balance-sheet and off-balance-sheet assets needed to be in business. If one examines the company's behavior toward the longer-lived, on-balance-sheet assets (fundamentally property, plant, and equipment), the overwhelming percentage of money is invested to *maintain* them. Some of this "investment" takes the form of maintenance that is expensed by the accounting system. Yet, expenditures capitalized as investment do not add much as a percentage to the net fixed-assets base after current year depreciation.

The same is true of longer-lived, off-balance-sheet assets such as the product portfolio, distribution system, and the company's human organization. Most of the money invested each year in these assets is needed just to maintain them at their current level of competitive viability. However, almost all the investment in these assets is made through overhead cost accounts. Not only are these expenditures virtually all expensed (as is plant and equipment maintenance) but also it is difficult to even know which assets are receiving what level of investment[1] let alone if the total "investment" has been adequate. In spite of this lack of knowledge, these overhead costs are the target of "cost control" as it is done by modern financial managers. (Almost everyone seems to understand that it is not possible to squeeze direct labor and material costs through a senior management mandate.)

However, *just as in maintaining the company's physical assets, the least expensive way to maintain the off-balance-sheet assets is to do so currently.* Dollars not currently spent can have a very high negative return (as reported by the income statement) in a relatively short period of time. How much negative effect in how short a time depends on:

- The amount of investment required in each time period.
- The rate at which the productivity of the off-balance-sheet assets decays when they are not maintained.
- The amount of underinvesting.

The failure to invest, places immediate negative pressure on sales and costs (as recorded in the accounting system). The trade-offs can be terrible. In a company with 50 percent fixed costs (most would have more), one-half of every incremental sales dollar falls to the bottom line. How much product-development or distribution-system maintenance can be deferred and make it pay[2] even a year later? As in the case of physical assets, each succeeding accounting period continues to pay the price until the asset is restored.

What is much worse, however, is the increased amount of investment and business risk incurred when the company attempts to restore its undermaintained assets. As in the case of physical assets, it can take a high level of investment to restore an undermaintained off-balance-sheet asset. For example, restoring a market position means *gaining* share. Most managers would agree that it takes much more investment,

---

[1] How many companies tell you how much they spent maintaining or augmenting their market position last year, let alone how much was new investment as opposed to maintenance?

[2] I.e., costs go down more than incremental profits from lost sales do.

made at greater risk, to gain market share than it does to maintain a current position. What will it cost the U.S. automobile industry to regain its former market share? Is it worth the investment and risk to try?

Said simply, there is no advantage, even in the time frame of a few years, in undermaintaining the company's off-balance-sheet assets. While it cannot record the off-balance-sheet investments in a time period, the financial system can reflect a lack of investment, as current period sales and costs are hurt by a failure to invest in previous periods.

There is one *temporary* way out. A company can continue to undermaintain its off-balance-sheet assets. However, because of the effect of previous undermaintenance on current-year results, it must underspend at an accelerating rate. In effect, a company can liquidate its off-balance-sheet assets through the income statement just as it can its physical assets. The difference is that because assets are not on the balance sheet, their liquidation is invisible to readers of the financial statements.

This is in fact how many American companies that had good market franchises and product portfolios have been critically weakened. In many cases, the reported earnings of these companies collapsed long after their competitive viability had been lost; they had been sustained by the invisible liquidation of their off-balance-sheet assets through the income statement.

Assuming one has no interest in such a doomsday scenario, financial management, no matter how benign, is still not a good way to manage the maintenance of the off-balance-sheet assets. *Managing hundreds or even thousands of daily activities, which make up the maintenance of the off-balance-sheet assets, through an overall financial plan is really "non-management" of these activities.* The overhead costs through which these investments are made are reflected in the financial plan as expenditures *by responsibility* in a *time period* (usually per month). Managers cannot possibly know how these funds are used on a daily basis.

Improved control of real business activities, particularly overhead activities, gives management much more control over the long-run, short-run trades being made as the company invests in its off-balance-sheet assets. It is the current management approach, which never deals with these investment decisions in any detail, that is out of control.

ANALOGUES STILL HAVE THE SAME LIMITATIONS

It is important to remember that all the limitations discussed in Chapter 1 apply to any new analogues. New analogues *tell managers what they can and nothing more*. It is very important not to fall right back into the analogue management trap by believing any measure can be more than a *very* limited reflection of a given business reality.

To avoid this problem, managers need to remind themselves that they must understand *why* things happen, not just *what* happened. *Analogues in general cannot answer the question "Why?" well at all*. Yet the action managers take normally requires that they have some view as to why something has occurred.

CHAPTER 7

GETTING THE MANAGEMENT REPORTS RIGHT

Conceiving of new analogue measures does not yield positive results if they are used in the wrong ways. Chapter 5 pointed out some ways in which accounting data is currently used in a technically improper fashion. To illustrate the point, three examples of reports using accounting data were used:

- Product costing.
- Expense budgeting.
- Customer profitability reporting, as both a measure of customer profitability and as a control report.

This chapter attempts to describe the principles that *must* be followed in any analogue reporting scheme to avoid making similar technical mistakes, whether the data comes from the accounting system, the production process, or even from outside the company. Because most readers will be more familiar with them, reports using accounting data will be used to illustrate these principles. In the process, solutions to the problems presented in Chapter 5 will emerge.

There are a number of technical and business management problems involved in creating a good management information system. The most central of these is to understand that it is *essential to separate the reporting of data into two major classifications:*

- Data to be used for better understanding the business.
- Data to be used for controlling the business.

Data for understanding the business includes the various measurements a company may choose to make in order to help management better *understand* such issues as the following:

- Product cost.
- Location profitability.
- Customer profitability.
- Product line profitability.

Control systems are intended to motivate management behavior to attain reasonable objectives. The following are examples of control reporting:

- Profitability against a profit plan.
- Expense against budgets.
- Sales revenue against targets.

The best technical solutions to these two reporting problems make it nearly impossible to use the same techniques for both purposes even though the basic data used may be identical. Companies often try to combine both approaches with indifferent, and frequently quite negative results. When negative results occur, they tend to concentrate in the long-term areas of the business and, therefore, have a serious impact.

On the positive side, when the measurement and control issues are handled well, the underlying purpose for combining both systems—the desire to "control" such issues as product line profitability for example—is actually enhanced.

MANAGEMENT-CONTROL SYSTEMS

The essence of good management-control reporting is to report actual performance against preassigned targets by responsibility in an unambiguous and technically defensible manner. To achieve this level of reporting, the following things are necessary:

- *Each* cost or revenue account must be the responsibility of a *single* executive.

- All costs or revenue recorded in that account must be under the *control* of that responsible executive.
- Control *targets* for that account must be fair.

A good control system must solve problems such as:

- Several organizations may play a role in acquiring a portion of a single source of revenue. (Most customer revenue in a bank has this characteristic.)
- Some costs vary with the amount of volume a unit handles. The services are often performed for other internal departments, thus the causes of the volume are not under the direct control of the processing unit; for example, data processing.
- Some costs are shared between organizations in a time period (i.e., "loaning" employees).
- Some costs are out of management's control in the short run. (Leases are a good example.)

The following approaches are used to solving these problems:

- Transfer pricing.
- Cost allocations.
- Multiple credit for revenue.

Unfortunately they frequently cause more problems than they solve when elements are introduced into the control system that are completely beyond the manager's control. Also, the methods used are often indefensible.

When one examines the underlying reasons for including elements in the control systems that are not controlled by the unit itself, there is frequently a desire to control not only responsibility but also other elements of the business such as customer profitability. The result, unfortunately, is that neither is actually controlled effectively.

MEASUREMENT SYSTEMS

For various strategic and tactical reasons, a business needs to have information about a variety of subjects:

- Product costs.
- The costs of supplying various services.
- Product-line volume and profitability.
- Customer profitability.
- Geographic area profitability.

In order to measure these well, we must deal with a number of technical and management issues such as:

- Assigning revenue to revenue sources (customer versus product line versus geography).
- Understanding how to regard the costs of an element that is being measured, especially how to handle costs that vary, but not proportionately, as the volume of a product or of a service activity grows; costs that are necessary to produce a product or a service activity but do not vary with its volume; and costs that are necessary to an activity but will not "go away" if the activity is eliminated.
- Deciding how to measure varying levels of detail for various management purposes.
- Settling the question of using actual costs and revenue versus budgeted amounts. (Is performance variance really a strategic product-line or geographic-profitability issue?)

RELATIONSHIP BETWEEN CONTROL AND MANAGEMENT

How are these two activities related? The central issue is responsibility. In most cases companies are not organized by customer or product lines. In addition, even when companies are organized geographically, there are revenues that are partially the result of activities beyond the geographic area and costs incurred by others for the benefit of the local geographic organization.

Therefore, it is very difficult to meet the responsibility criteria mentioned in the definition of a good control system. However, a good control system has, by definition, a complete set of targets for all the revenue and expenses of the company. It is possible, therefore, using the proper approach, to do some sophisticated *measurement* by using *targets in the control systems. The important point to recognize is that control against these targets occurs in the control system and not in the measurement system* that is being used to support strategic and tactical decisions such as product-line modification or pricing.

A couple of simple examples may be helpful in illustrating the two concepts of control and measurement and their interrelationships. Manufacturing company examples will be used because they present a full range of the conditions that must be covered. Therefore, the conditions that arise in a bank, an insurance company, or another service company are covered, as are the examples of commonly made errors described in Chapter 5.

COST CONTROL IN MANUFACTURING

The costs of a manufacturing company can be divided into two broad categories:

- Factory costs.
- Selling and administrative costs.

Factory costs are generally those costs incurred within production facilities to support the production process and are the costs that are transferred into inventory under IRS regulations and Generally Accepted Accounting Principles (GAAP). Selling and administrative costs and all other costs are treated as period costs (i.e., they are not inventoried).

Under our definition of control, every dollar of cost in both broad categories must be categorized as the responsibility of a single executive. Further, these costs must be compared to a cost target that is also the sole responsibility of the same executive.

It is quite possible to do this in the control area if the following three principles are followed:

- Define an organizational structure (i.e., a set of "cost centers," each having a *single* responsible manager).
- For each manager so designated, assign a set of accounts for collecting costs which will only contain costs that he actually controls.
- Have a target that is "fair" for each of these accounts. Besides being reasonable, this could mean that the target is *flexible* (i.e., the budget goes up or down, if the costs being put in that account are affected by the level of production).

Before we go into our mythical company and apply these principles to its factory costs, *it is important to emphasize we are only discussing controlling these costs. For the moment, we are ignoring the measurement issues such as product costing.* These issues will be dealt with after we have covered the control problem.

Controlling Factory Costs

Let's proceed to the factory where we want to control the costs. Like most factories of any size, this factory can be divided into two types of departments, direct and indirect. Direct departments are production departments and the indirect departments "service" the direct departments with such things as material handling, tool processing, maintenance, and warehousing.

If we examine one of these direct production departments, such as a stamping department, we will see that the costs that are incurred can, themselves, be divided into direct and indirect costs. This is true even though the department is a direct department.

Direct costs are those incurred in the department as part of the actual production process. They generally include material consumed in stamping out the department's product and labor used in operating the presses. These costs are usually referred to as direct labor and direct material costs.

The department has a number of cost accounts (10 to 20 would not be uncommon) that are indirect even though they are incurred in a direct department. These costs include items such as the salary of the department foreman, worker fringe benefits, and other departmental expenses such as gloves, lubricants, or contracted services such as training or maintenance. The department's performance against its direct costs targets is usually reported daily or weekly. The indirect cost performance is reported less often, usually monthly. Now let's apply our three principles to this department.

The first principle says that only one executive at a time can be responsible. In our mythical press department this is normally the foreman. What happens when the department runs two shifts and there are two foremen, one for each shift? If this occurs, reporting must be by shift. Another approach is to start the reporting process at the next management level and use the general foreman to whom they both report. When this occurs, the general foreman would be the single responsible executive. If we report once per day and do not choose one responsible foreman, we have lost control—no matter how accurate the reporting. Since no single person is responsible, the foremen can blame the variances on each other rather than actually explain them.

The second principle says that costs should be charged for control purposes to the manager who controls them. In a one-shift operation the foreman is responsible for those costs that he actually "spends" or controls. In general, this means that all costs fall into his cost accounts without being allocated to him. For example, the direct labor and direct material consumed in his department is under his control. Indirect costs such as employee fringe benefits, which follow direct labor, and the consumable materials and purchased services we referred to earlier are also under his control because he must authorize their use.

Plant costs such as utilities are often allocated to press departments. Since after all, they *use* the utilities, don't they? Yes, *but they don't control them*! According to our principles of control, these costs should belong to the person actually incurring them, probably the plant engineer. This principle can be seen from two perspectives, actual control and the ability to explain variances.

As was explained in Chapter 5, the plant engineer has a much better basis for actually controlling these costs than the users have. He not only controls the fundamental supply decisions but also has a much better technical understanding than they do. Usage of heat, light, and power is going on all over the facility in various ways. Most users represent a small portion of the total usage. There is a need for someone with an overall view of the cost to control it and to explain variances.

If the press room is using too much power because they leave their presses running or have different equipment than was planned in the budgeting process, the plant engineer is in a much better position to evaluate the additional costs in terms of power and make a variance explanation that can lead to real corrective action.

On the other hand, if we ask our press department foreman to explain why he exceeded his target for heat, light, and power, he will probably say he was surprised to see the variance. He will point out that he put the amount provided by the plant engineer in his budget, and that he doesn't understand the basis of allocation anyway.

These principles apply to most other costs that are allocated (i.e., data processing). Better control obviously results from budgeting and controlling where costs are actually incurred:

- The spender almost always has the pricing control of the cost.
- When companies are tempted to allocate, there are almost always several users, none of whom has a good view of the overall cost.
- Abuse by users can be better observed and resolved by the service supplier.
- The allocation methods available are technically questionable.

The third principle of control is the need for fair targets. The most important issue here is to be sure that costs that vary with the volume of the cost center's output have flexible targets.

Let's return to our press department and look at the targets against which our foreman is being measured. His direct labor and direct material targets probably come from product standards. That is, he "earns" so much direct labor and direct material costs per unit of output of physical product. At the end of each shift, the output is reported to the accounting department, which converts it into the targets against which the actual usage of labor hours and materials are compared and a favorable or unfavorable variance is computed. If these standards are "correct," they meet both the criteria of the third principle—they are "fair" and they are flexible (i.e., they go up as he produces more output).

But what about the targets for the department's 10 to 20 indirect-cost accounts? Here one sees a variety of approaches, almost none of which are correct. That is, none fairly represent the proper target under the circumstances the way the departmental standards do for direct labor and material. This is easy to understand if one compares the expected behavior of these indirect costs against the methods used to set budgets or targets for them.

The most important characteristic of these "other" press department costs is that some of them tend to go up with the volume of production in the department while others do not. For example, the foreman's salary will tend to be consistent as man-hours are added to his shift while fringe benefits and glove usage will tend to rise. Also, cost accounts that go up with the volume of production do not all go up at the same rate. Some will tend to rise smoothly and directly with production while others will rise less rapidly or in "steps." Table 7-1 is intended to illustrate this phenomenon for any direct department.

The various production levels at which the department can operate are shown across the top of the table as percentages of "ideal" capacity. At 110 percent and 120 percent the department is using overtime. The various indirect cost accounts are shown down the side of the table. There are six costs that vary with the level of production and four "fixed" costs that do not.

If one examines the behavior of the variable costs as production increases, there is not a common pattern of increase. While they all move upward as production increases, some move with each increase and some do not. The fixed costs always stay the same, no matter what the level of production is. If his budgets for these accounts are to be fair measures of the expense our foreman needs to operate at these various production levels, the budgets need to reflect the amounts in Table 7-1.

The solution is of course obvious. In this day of the computer, Table 7-1 can be stored. At month-end the computer would then pick the proper budget amounts for each of the accounts from the table. The computer program would, of course, need to be supplied information about the level of production for the month so it would know which cells in the table to use. If the department operated between two of the levels shown on the table, for example at 85 percent of capacity, the amounts at 80 percent and 90 percent would be averaged. Other in-between percentages would likewise be determined through interpolation. *This approach has been called flexible budgeting.*

In my experience, as simple as this approach is, very few companies use it. Most seem to use cost targets that are fixed at what they believe will be the average production level over the year. If a variable budget is desired, these fixed budgets are divided by the average direct labor hours to get a "rate per direct labor hour." The actual hours worked each month are then multiplied by this rate to get the budget for that month, thereby making the budgets "flexible."

If this approach were not used so frequently, it would not be worth mentioning since it only gives a proper cost target when the department is operating exactly at the *projected* average. At any other level of production the target is seriously wrong and therefore useless as a control target. This approach is saying that all costs vary proportionally with volume. In fact, the costs in real departments behave much more like the examples in Table 7-1.

Interestingly, the reason many people give for using a fixed rate per hour for these budgets is the need to have anoverhead rate for cost accounting purposes. This is a classic

TABLE 7-1
(Monthly cost for each account at varying levels of production.)

				Direct Department I Indirect Cost			
Volume Level	60%	70%	80%	90%	100%	110%	120%
Cost Type							
Overtime Premium						5,000	10,000
Indirect production materials	$ 6,000	$ 7,000	$ 8,000	$ 9,000	$10,000	$11,000	$12,000
Samples	2,000	2,000	3,000	3,000	4,000	4,000	5,000
Consumable tooling	4,000	4,500	4,500	5,000	5,500	5,500	6,000
Minor equipment items	1,400	1,400	1,400	1,700	1,700	1,700	2,000
Office supplies	600	700	800	900	1,000	1,100	1,200
Total Variable Cost	$14,000	15,600	17,700	19,600	22,200	28,300	36,200
Foreman	5,200	5,200	5,200	5,200	5,200	5,200	5,200
Training	4,500	4,500	4,500	4,500	4,500	4,500	4,500
Equipment rental	3,000	3,000	3,000	3,000	3,000	3,000	3,000
Depreciation	8,000	8,000	8,000	8,000	8,000	8,000	8,000
Total Fixed Cost	$20,700	$20,700	$20,700	$20,700	$20,700	$20,700	$20,700
Total Department Budget	$34,700	$36,300	$38,400	$40,300	$42,900	$49,000	$56,900

case of confusing cost control with cost measurement and obtaining the usual results, a bad cost target and bad cost accounting.

I would like to complete my comments on the control of cost in our mythical factory. So far we have only dealt with the problem in *direct departments*. In these departments we have said we must be sure of the following things:

- That we have defined a cost center that is the responsibility of a single executive. (While this would usually be the first-level manager—the foreman—it need not be if a higher level executive is prepared to explain the variances.)
- That the cost accounts for this cost center only contain costs over which the responsible executive actually has primary control. (This almost always means those that he actually spends.)
- That the targets actually work technically (i.e., are fair under the circumstances). In direct departments, this means handling both "direct" costs and "indirect" costs that will vary in different ways as production increases or decreases.

In the rest of the plant we have indirect cost centers or departments. Some of these cost centers are blue-collar production support departments, such as material handling and the tool room, while others, such as plant industrial engineering and the plant manager's office, are not.

However, the costs in their budget reports tend to look like the indirect costs of the direct departments. The costs are salaries and wages, various materials, and purchased goods and services. Further, these costs behave like the indirect costs of the direct departments. While there will be an overall tendency for costs to rise with the level of volume in the plant, the behavior of the individual accounts will vary from being essentially "fixed" (i.e., volume insensitive), to being irregularly variable with volume.

Therefore, the flexible budgeting approach (Table 7-1) suggested for setting targets on the indirect costs of the direct departments can be used. The comments relative to single executive responsibility clearly apply, as do the comments relative to charging costs to the accounts of the "spending," rather than the "using" cost centers. That is, the rest of the factory can be managed for *cost control* in the same way the indirect costs of direct departments are handled. While the cost "drivers" for variable cost accounts are usually the volumes in the direct departments that each department is servicing, any appropriate measure of volume can be used.

Again, one does not see this "flexible" budgeting approach very often. Instead, one sees one of the two approaches we discussed for setting cost control targets for indirect costs in the direct departments:

- Fixed budgets for all accounts in all indirect departments based on an "expected" level of volume in the plan.
- Variable budgets based on a rate per direct labor in accounts that are believed to vary with plant volume in all of or some of the indirect departments.

The net effect, as in the direct departments, is to have technically incorrect budget amounts in any cost account that naturally varies with the level of production any time the plant is not operating at the planned volume.

In addition to having poor targets, it is usual to find some of the actual costs allocated. Since these departments are, by definition, "internal service" departments, one is tempted to charge the using department rather than the spending departments even if in some cases, the using departments are other indirect departments. *For control purposes this method should not be used. Costs should be charged and thereby controlled where they are spent.*

Controlling and Selling and Administrative Expense

Selling and administrative departments, including engineering, are like factory indirect departments for cost control

purposes. The three principles of a single responsible executive, costs under his control, and a fair target for each account,
of course still apply. The major difference involves the "cost
drivers" for any variable expenses these departments may
have. The proper driver is frequently not volume in the
factory. Instead it may be better to use things such as
customer orders received, invoices processed, and so forth.
Since these cost centers have much less variable expense, they
should be easier to budget. In fact, because the first two
principles are often violated, we often find the situation
described in Chapter 5 in these departments.

Cost Control in Service Industries

As I suggested earlier, manufacturing companies face the
broadest range of cost control technical problems. As a result,
the techniques previously illustrated will also cover the
service industries. Volume-sensitive costs in service companies can be covered by using the flexible budgeting approach.
Each department can have a budget similar to the one in
Table 7-1. If one measure of volume for all the variable
accounts is not appropriate, two or more can be used. There
can even be a separate volume indicator for each variable
account in a department if that is appropriate. For example, a
credit department may have some accounts that vary with the
number of customer orders processed and others that vary
with the level of collection activity, while others are fixed or
volume insensitive.

If a service company has an organization, such as a large
retail distribution center, it can control the costs as if the
organization were a factory; that is, use a combination of
production standards, flexible budgets, and fixed budgets as
appropriate.

Summary of Control

As was suggested at the beginning of this chapter, the
examples use accounting data, but the principles apply to

controlling against any analogue. For example, if we wish to control against a target level of production defects or sales order fulfillment, the same principles would apply.

It is also worthwhile to remind ourselves that in dealing with any analogue, it is very important to understand its limitations. In the case of control reporting, even if we do the reporting in a technically correct manner, we only know if the budget was exceeded or not. We don't know how *well* the budget was actually spent or really much else.

MEASURING PRODUCT COST IN MANUFACTURING

As in the case of cost control, manufacturing companies provide a good basis for discussing the problems faced when accounting data is used for *measurement* rather than control. Measuring the cost of producing products in these companies is a particularly good example. The following "cost accounting" discussion will deal with a number of measurement issues such as:

- The role of budgeted versus actual costs in the measurement process.
- A way of measuring incremental costs.
- The relationship of measurement and control.
- One solution to the cost accounting problem discussed in Chapter 5.

Now that we have a method for *controlling* the costs in our mythical factory, we can attempt to measure the manufacturing costs of individual products. *The problem in doing this is that we have collected costs not by product but rather by responsibility.* A system to reclassify these costs by product is now required.

The first logical question then is which costs should be assigned to each product? Should we use the actual costs or budgeted costs? While some managers would argue for using the actual costs incurred, most would agree that the target costs are the most logical ones to use in this reclassification process. If the actual costs are used, we will find the product costs varying randomly over time. In fact, the performance of our factory departments is varying for reasons that are not inherent to the product being produced at that time.

This is a fundamental principle. It is necessary to remove "performance" from the measurement process in most measurement cases. If a bank branch or a retail store location is not being adequately managed, that mismanagement is not a reason for relocating the office. The value of the location can be better understood by examining the location's profitability as if management were meeting targets that were fair in the circumstances.

But let's get back to our cost-measurement problem. The next question focuses on how the targets (budgets) can be used to determine product costs. In the direct departments, the direct costs (i.e., the direct labor and material expended in the actual production process) are not a major problem. The targets typically used, the standard labor and materials cost, *are by product* and, therefore, no reclassification is necessary.[1]

However, the targets for *indirect costs* in the *direct departments are not by product*. Further, all the targets in the indirect departments are handled in the same fashion. These budgets look like Table 7-1 and are definitely collected by responsibility.

The usual procedure used to reclassify these overhead costs was described in Chapter 5 and is repeated here. The first step is to assign the indirect departments costs to the direct departments based on the levels of service supplied (Figure 7-1).

---

[1]The fact that the direct labor and direct material standards happen to be by product is pure good luck. When we used them in the control system, we were only interested in their ability to help us create targets by responsibility (foreman) for these costs. The fact that they are also by product comes from the way in which they are constructed (i.e., so much labor or material per "good" unit produced.) Because the total cost for the product, including overhead, that we are now attempting to compute is also called "standard cost," some people are confused and believe standard *product* costs are somehow used as control targets.

FIGURE 7-1

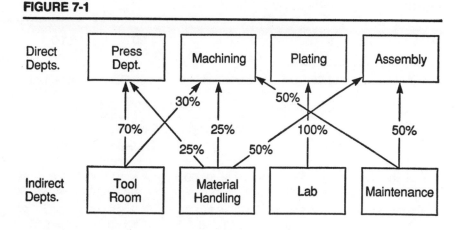

Then assign all the indirect cost that is incurred within the direct departments and that which is assigned (the indirect department cost) to the products. The usual method of assignment uses the direct labor hours of each of the products in each of the direct departments. A rate per direct labor hour is used for each direct department that is large enough to assign all the overhead incurred by it and assign to it, to the products that are expected to pass through that direct department (Figure 7-2).

I previously criticized this process because it has the effect of transferring *all* factory costs to the products. In fact, most of this factory indirect cost is not volume sensitive[2] and that which is volume sensitive usually does not increase in proportion to the direct labor hours (level of production). The net result is to derive a product cost that is overstated leading to some serious management mistakes.

How then do we deal with this problem? The issue still involves the transfer of overhead incurred in both the direct and indirect factory departments to the products. However, *the goal is to transfer only the amount of overhead that increases as plant volume increases* (i.e., the incremental overhead to go with the direct labor and direct material that

[2]As long as the company owns the plant and operates it at all.

FIGURE 7-2

Dir. Labor Rate	8.00	9.00	11.00	5.00
Overhead Rates per DLH	15.00/DLH	12.00/DLH	18.00/DLH	8.00/DLH

Product A

Press Dept. .5 DLH	Machining 1.0 DLH	Plating .2 DLH	Assembly 2.0 DLH

Dir. Labor Cost	.5× $8.00 = $4.00	1.0 × $9.00 = $9.00	.2 × $11.00 = $2.20	2.0 × $5.00 = $10.00
Overhead Cost	.5× $15.00 = $7.50	1.0 × $12.00 = $12.00	.2 × $18.00 = $3.60	2.0 × $8.00 = $16.00

Product cost of Product A
Direct labor   4.00 + 9.00 + 2.20 + 10.00 = $25.20
Direct material   30.00
Overhead   7.50 + 12.00 + 3.60 + 16.00 =   39.10

                                               $94.30/100 units

is incremented by definition). This can be achieved by using the flexible budget tables.

If you look at the tables (such as Table 7-1) that describe the behavior of each indirect cost in the individual direct departments and add up *all* the variable accounts for each level of volume, you will find the relationship of that departments' total indirect costs to overall volume in the plant.

Table 7-1 is reproduced as Table 7-2. The calculation at the bottom shows the rate at which the total of all indirect costs in our mythical Press Department go up with production in that department.

As was discussed earlier, every other *direct department* has a similar table and therefore a similar calculation can be made. If an *indirect department* has costs that increase with plant volume, then the same calculation can be made showing the relationship of that department's costs to plant volume.

TABLE 7-2
(Monthly cost for each account at varying levels of production).

| | | | | Direct Department 1 | | | |
| | | | | Indirect Cost | | | |
Volume Level	60%	70%	80%	90%	100%	110%	120%
Cost Type							
Overtime Premium						5,000	10,000
Indirect production							
material	$ 6,000	$ 7,000	$ 8,000	$ 9,000	$10,000	$11,000	$12,000
Overtime samples	2,000	2,000	3,000	3,000	4,000	4,000	5,000
Consumable tooling	**4,000**	**4,500**	**4,500**	**5,000**	**5,500**	**5,500**	**6,000**
Minor equipment items	1,400	1,400	1,400	1,700	1,700	1,700	2,000
Office supplies	600	700	800	900	1,000	1,100	1,200
Total Variable Cost	$14,000	15,600	17,700	19,600	22,200	28,300	36,200
Foreman	5,200	5,200	5,200	5,200	5,200	5,200	5,200
Training	4,500	4,500	4,500	4,500	4,500	4,500	4,500
Equipment rental	3,000	3,000	3,000	3,000	3,000	3,000	3,000
Depreciation	8,000	8,000	8,000	8,000	8,000	8,000	8,000
Total Fixed Cost	$20,700	$20,700	$20,700	$20,700	$20,700	$20,700	$20,700
Total Department Budget	$34,700	$36,300	$38,400	$40,300	$42,900	$49,000	$56,900

$$\frac{\$28,300 - \$17,700}{110\% - 80\%} = \$353 \text{ increase in cost per 1\% increase in production}$$

(The table extends from the 60% to the 120% level of production. The calculation was made in the narrower range of 80% to 110% because this is the rate at which the plant usually operates). Only the totals of the variable costs at these levels were used.

113

We have captured the way in which overhead varies with production in the plant! Further, we have captured how it *should* vary because we are using the *budgeted* amounts just as we do for direct labor and direct material. Normally, these costs for each direct and indirect department would be expressed as a rate per direct labor hour.

One can then go through the procedures described in Figures 7-1 and 7-2 only using that portion of the indirect cost that varies with volume. That is, a variable cost rate for direct labor hours is determined for each direct department that is sufficient to assign all the variable indirect cost of that direct department plus any variable costs assigned from the indirect departments that service it. *The rest of the indirect cost is never applied to the products.* It is treated as a period cost because it is! Standard product cost is then:

Direct material – From product standards
Direct labor   – From product standards
Overhead   – *Total* of all departmental variable costs per direct labor hour multiplied by standard direct labor hours in this product.

This methodology says that a product has directly identifiable costs—direct labor, direct material, and some overhead costs—that are caused because the product causes plant volume. Presumably, any other product of the same volume, as expressed in direct labor hours, would cause the same volume-related expense to occur.

Some writers have criticized the continuing use of direct labor hours as a means of relating factory overhead to individual products because the proportion of direct labor to total product costs has declined to such a low level in American manufacturing companies. (From possibly 40 percent to 5 to 10 percent). I am not opposed to other measures of volume if appropriate ones can be found. Direct labor hours have been used in this example in the belief that most readers would be more comfortable with them. In fact, the subject of cost accounting is a much more complex issue than this example which is included to illustrate the broader issue of incremented costs as a concern in the measurement process.

Failure to include all overhead costs in product costs will disturb some American accountants for at least two reasons:

- Product costs would not properly represent the amount of cost that must be "covered" by prices.
- The amount of factory costs transferred to inventory would be too small. This violates GAAP and IRS regulations and could result in understated profits.

But what about the fact that the extra cost we would be including in product cost would not "go away" if we ceased to produce our product? Can a cost that does not disappear with a product really be a product cost? If it is not product cost what is it? It is a cost of being in business just as much as is the president's salary. Furthermore, if we confuse product costs and being-in-business costs we are prone to make mistakes every time we make a measurement that uses product costs. Furthermore, we do this routinely when we do product or product line profitability or customer profitability.

The inventory-valuation issue can be handled with a journal entry monthly or whenever an income statement is being prepared. Such an entry will also satisfy the IRS if it is properly done. *Getting the inventory "right" can hardly be an argument for getting all the product costs wrong.*

Summary of Measurement

By its very nature, measurement reporting is a much broader issue than control reporting. Because of this, it is more difficult to summarize. However, the following points are worth a brief discussion:

- The limits of measurement.
- The use of budgets versus actual experience.
- The role of allocation and incremental costs.
- The relationship to control.

The Limits of Measurement

Unlike control reporting, which is very much a focused activity,[3] the only limitation on the measurements that management may choose to make is the scope of its imagination. Further, there is no need to be confined to measurements using accounting data. In fact, measurements that do not use accounting data may be more valuable because they can be closer to the actual business functions.

However, because of the "wide open" characteristic of measurement, it is much easier to make mistakes. It is very important to remember the following:

- It is necessary to understand the *limitations* of the measurement; remember, it is just another analogue.
- *No* measurement can really report *why* something is happening.
- It is not necessary to *measure* (as opposed to control) things *routinely* unless the fundamentals require it. For example, because sales are an important variable in measuring customer profitability, it needs to be a routine (i.e., capture all the transactions) measurement. However, many measurements can be made as special studies often using budgets rather than actual data.

Use of Budget Versus Actual

It is very important to separate what *should* happen from what *is* happening or did happen in making measurements. As in the case of product costs, using actual costs can cause random variations in, say, branch profitability, that have no value in making the kinds of decisions for which most measurements are made. This confuses many people because they believe they can control to measurements. Once one understands this is rarely possible, the good news becomes clear (i.e., *because you are using budgets, you can make measurements whenever you want to*).

---

[3]After all, there is only one organization to be controlled.

For example, those people who are interested in more elaborate forms of product costing do *not* have to install new accounting systems to collect actual costs in different ways after all. Various schemes can be tried on a special study basis using budget data. Remember, control against these budgets occurs in the control system and control problems must be dealt with by using that system.

The Role of Allocation and Incremental Costs

It is perfectly suitable to use allocation in measurement systems as long as one understands the difference between costs (and even revenues) that will change with a particular decision and those that won't.

A good idea is to make calculations both ways. Most American businesses have more fixed costs than they realize, probably because they don't measure them carefully. There is also a tendency to use fixed costs without understanding the volume and flexibility issues involved.

THE RELATIONSHIP TO CONTROL

There is no error more ubiquitous in preparing American management reports than confusing measurement and control. This is usually done because we wish to control to a measurement. The frequency with which this problem is encountered in American management reports and the damage that is caused compels these summary statements:

- Unless the conditions for control are present, it is *not* possible to use measurements in control reports.
- Control to a measurement *is* still possible if we are willing to hold a group of executives responsible. (For example, to reduce the cost of a product or increase the speed with which customer orders are processed.)

Given the focus on analogue management in the American management system, one would expect a great deal of discussion of the technical issues involved. In fact, this is not the case. If it were, we might not only have management information that is more technically correct, but also and more importantly, we might be much more aware of the limitations of the analogues that are used.

CHAPTER 8

MANAGING THE LARGEST
SINGLE COST—OVERHEAD

Managing overhead costs more effectively is the single best short-term competitive opportunity most companies have. In many cases, American companies can *materially increase their competitive capability and significantly reduce their costs at the same time.*

Overhead is the largest single cost in American companies. Even factory costs are usually more than 50 percent overhead despite the need to pay for the direct material and labor used in actually making the products. There is no question that overhead as a percentage of all costs is rising. In manufacturing, overhead is increasing because mechanization is replacing direct labor. In the overall economy, the growth of services as a percentage of all output has directly contributed to the same trend. Many American white-collar workers also represent overhead. (Between 1978 and 1985 the number of white-collar workers rose by 10 million to about 58 million, while blue-collar employment dropped 1.9 million to about 30 million.)

There is also little question that we experience a great deal of trouble managing overhead. This difficulty is causing a drag on the productivity of individual companies and in the overall economy. One study by Morgan Stanley, the investment bank, shows that between 1978 and 1984 white-collar productivity actually declined by almost 10 percent. The study shows blue-collar productivity rose 13 percent during this same period. Yet many believe more was invested in white-collar productivity than in blue-collar on a per-worker basis.

WHAT IS OVERHEAD?

Most people define *overhead* as "costs incurred in support of the company's main revenue-generating activities—producing products or supplying services (or both)." However, when one tries to be more precise, a number of issues arise. The white-collar/blue-collar distinction poses the problem of including a number of factory service departments, such as a tool room or plant security as direct expense while counting the tellers in a bank as overhead.

Another approach to defining overhead would be to count those costs incurred to support internal operations as overhead and those costs incurred to supply the company's customers as direct. However, many internal support costs are quite central to producing the products or servicing the customer; such as quality control costs in a plant or the updating of the customers' checking account ledgers in a bank.

A more useful distinction might be fixed (i.e., volume-insensitive) costs versus variable costs (i.e., those costs that change with the volume of production or sales if the company is a service company). Presumably those costs must have a direct connection to output since they vary with it. Many of the "fixed" costs in a company, though, are quite central to the production or customer-service activities. Examples would be production foremen and equipment deprecation in a plant or the lease payment for a branch office of a bank.

In spite of this, I am choosing fixed costs as the definition of overhead. That is, *overhead* means "any expense account for which the company does not use engineered standards or other measures of output as the basis of its budget (*i.e., those costs that are fixed or are budgeted as if they are fixed*)." In a manufacturing company, this would define every plant cost except direct labor and direct material and cost accounts having "flexible" budgets,[1] as overhead. All the other cost centers such as engineering, sales, and administration, unless they had flexible budgets, would also be overhead, regardless of the importance of their role in servicing the customer.

In a service company as well, all costs would be overhead except those that have an output-based budget. For example, in a retail company that uses engineered standards in its distribution center and "sales clerk scheduling" geared to expected customer traffic in its stores, the costs covered by these "standards" would be direct. Everything else would be overhead. Likewise, in a bank only those costs covered by a flexible budget such as a teller scheduling system would be direct.

WHY OVERHEAD IS DIFFICULT TO CONTROL

This approach focuses on why the analogue management system has trouble managing overhead. Costs that can be controlled using output-based budgets fit well into our analogue management system. Those that are not amenable to this technique are troublesome.

Analogue management is limited by the validity of the analogues used as representations of the business activity that we wish to measure or control. Control, as we saw in Chapter 7, is a question of controlling actual performance against a predetermined target by responsibility. The degree to which the target is an accurate representation of the *business activity* we wish to accomplish is a major determiner of the analogue's effectiveness as a control tool.

In those areas of expense where output-based budgeting can be used, a target that is a measure of actual output produced can be used. While this approach has some prob-

---

[1] As defined in Chapter 7, these are budgets that vary with the level of production but not necessarily in direct proportion, as a standard does.

lems, it moves the analogue measure closer to the business activity we are trying to control (i.e., the expense required to produce a given output).

Overhead as defined is not and, in most cases, cannot be controlled using this approach. The "products" that are the output of overhead expense cannot be precisely defined. Our solution to this problem tends to focus on controlling overhead expense against budgets that are time-based instead of output-based (i.e., so much budget per month). *We then measure expenditures against these time-period budgets and declare victory. In fact, we have taken a giant step away from control when budgets no longer represent real business activities. These budgets are merely limitations on input.*

It can be argued that the users of the outputs of the various overhead cost centers are a control against their failure to produce. However, user control is hard to enforce since a supplying organization provides a myriad of services to several "users."

Furthermore, the time-budgeting process itself does not rest on a rational determination of service-level expectations by an organization. In most organizations it is merely the lowest level allocation of a corporate-level expense target. Most companies allocate the amount of overhead cost that they feel they can afford and still make their profit target, to the various functional organizations (i.e., sales, engineering, etc.). The cost centers within each of the functional organizations eventually receive a share of the budget against which their expenditures are controlled. The normal way this allocation is accomplished is to begin with the status quo (i.e., last year) and attempt to adjust the allocation based on the increased or decreased amount of money available modified by a perception of the changing requirements of the various cost centers.

In some companies the allocation of funds turns into an elaborate negotiation. One tactic frequently used is for the lower-level organizational units to submit inflated budgets, expecting them to be cut by senior management. When senior management reduces the budget, both sides can feel their goals have been accomplished.

Because this process does not focus on the actual overhead activities themselves and is the byproduct of a negotiation:

- There is no assurance that the available budget has been properly "spread" across the various organizational units.
- There is a "natural creep" in overhead costs during years of corporate prosperity.

In leaner years, when profits become unsatisfactory, many companies either allocate less overhead to the various functional units or cut the budgets during the year. Midyear reductions are often done in such an arbitrary fashion that they do not increase the efficiency with which the remaining overhead funds are spent. Since most overhead costs that can be reduced in the short run are employee-related, these expenses tend to be reduced first, often with significant damage to employee loyalty and enthusiasm.

Simply stated, *the analogue management system does a poor job of managing the largest corporate expense. Other than being a good way of targeting an overall level of expense, the current system does little to manage either the allocation of overhead expenditure levels or the efficiency with which the funds are actually spent.*

Many managers do not understand the serious nature of this problem. They are quite confident that by managing to a total dollar target, they have effective control of overhead. If this approach really works, why do companies have to "cut" their overhead budgets so frequently? They do not do this with direct labor and direct material. It is also worth noting that the management literature focuses on how to reduce overhead or how it can be permanently made lower. Rarely, if ever, do we discuss managing overhead *activities* on a routine basis.

OVERHEAD EXPENSE HAS A NATURAL TENDENCY TO GROW

Managing overhead expense starts by understanding that it has a natural tendency to grow faster than the company's revenue growth. There are a number of reasons for this:

- Overhead services are supplied without cost to users within the corporation and to outsiders.
- Overhead suppliers have an incentive to try to increase their budgets even if the demand for their services is not increasing.
- Overhead services are frequently supplied through and to a network of organizational relationships that make it difficult to understand the cost/benefit relationships that result.

Overhead Services are Free

In general, overhead services within a corporation are supplied without direct cost to the users. There is no practical way to avoid this situation, although "cross-charging" can be useful in specific cases.[2] Because their services are free, most internal service functions are resource-bound. The more competently they perform in the eyes of their customers, the more demand they will usually experience.

Market-driven "signals" and incentives, indispensable to the corporation in its dealings with the outside world, are not available to help manage the supplying of internal services. When it supplies products to the outside market, the corporation receives information (signals) from the market about how much of which product to produce, as customers express their preferences through their buying decisions. Since the customer must pay for

---

[2] In Chapter 5, it was pointed out that overhead cost cannot be controlled this way. That is not to say that in specific instances, a pricing system cannot be used to restrain demand for a particular service even though responsibility for controlling the expense, of necessity, remains with its supplier. An example might be the use of a typing pool or graphics service.

the product he purchases there is an automatic control on the customers' demand. The customers' choices are thus affected by their perception of price versus value. The corporation also has an incentive to improve the product's performance or stop supplying those products rejected by the market.

Since overhead services are essentially free, the users of services such as data processing, accounting, and personnel have no limitation on their demand for services other than their own perception of internal needs. The real rationing or resource allocation must be done by the supplier of overhead services.

Because the users of overhead services do not send a revenue "signal" to the supplier, the service supplier does not see what the corporation sees as he attempts to allocate limited resources between the various corporate divisions or departments. Which special study is more important for accounting to do? For whom? Which systems' maintenance should data processing do and which should it defer?

What about the incentive to improve the efficiency with which some, or all, of the services are delivered? One would think that since they are "sold out" most of the time, overhead departments would have an incentive to deliver their services more efficiently. This is only partially true. When your product is selling well you don't normally try to improve it. Most managers in this situation try to get more resources to supply the endless demand. Just as the corporation could not increase its efficiency in supplying product enough for it to continue to raise output without more revenue, the internal organization does not see improving its efficiency as a major source of increased capacity. As a result, rather than attempt to improve efficiency, cost centers use their sold-out condition as a reason for acquiring more resources (i.e., a higher budget).

Overhead Suppliers Have Incentives to Increase Their Budgets

There are a number of reasons why an organization supplying overhead services will try to increase its budget:

- It perceives itself at capacity and usually interprets this as reflecting the value of its services rather than the fact that the services are free.
- In most corporations, there are a number of benefits that come to a growing organization that do not come to those that agree to stay the same size or get smaller. (Who ever heard of a manager's pay being increased as a direct result of his shrinking his organization?)
- Most organizations feel their budgets are barely adequate to provide the current level of service. A budget increase is often viewed as a means to create a margin of safety, reducing the chance that they will disappoint the organizations which use their services and suffer the resulting consequences.
- The competitive process used to determine the budgets of the various cost centers requirers organizations to continually press for budget increases, whether they need them or not.
- The managers of most cost centers overvalue their services based on limited knowledge of activities in the rest of the corporation (and human nature!).

The net effect of this situation is to produce a continual upward pressure on overhead budgets quite independent of the corporation's need for these services or its ability to pay for them.

Overhead Services are Supplied and Consumed in a Complex Network of Relationships

Overhead is used to support almost all of the corporation's activities. (Even, the direct manufacturing departments have overhead expense.) Therefore, it supports a large number of very complex relationships. In the context of our current control systems, the unit supplying services is an individual cost center. Depending on how management decides to create cost centers, there can be dozens and even hundreds of them in company. These cost centers use their budgets to supply various services to each other and to the outside world.[3] In order to understand the efficiency with which a company is using its overhead expenditures one needs to understand the costs and benefits to the corporation of these complex relationships.

WHY ACROSS-THE-BOARD CUTS DO NOT WORK

As we have seen, the modern American manager is faced with a dilemma as he attempts to manage overhead with the available tools. On the one hand, he is faced with the inevitable upward creep in overhead expenses caused by the factors discussed previously. On the other hand, he does not have a routine way of managing overhead except his time-based budgeting system which supplies no insight into the details of the myriad relationships he must understand to manage overhead expenditures at a more detailed level.

An approach frequently used to solve this problem is a mandated, across-the-board percentage cut in overhead budgets. All organizations are usually told they must reduce their expenditures by the same percentage, say 5 to 10 percent. These are the assumptions underlying this approach:

- It is impossible to really understand the overhead expenditure problem in a cost-effective way.
- "Fat" exists in the system that can be safely removed without harming the company's operations.
- Each overhead cost center will instinctively reduce its least effective spending, thereby improving the efficiency with which the remaining overhead dollars are used. Therefore, the overall "service level" will not decline and may even improve.
- If any organization cannot safely remove the mandated percentage reduction from its operation, it will com-

---

[3] Customers yes, but also vendors, lenders, investors, regulators, etc.

plain. A more detailed examination can then be made, and an exception granted, if one is warranted.

While it seems reasonable on the surface, this approach like most "shortcuts" in business, is flawed. It will usually produce a successful short-run cost reduction, often close to management's real target.[4] However, costs reduced this way have a tendency to "snap back." This occurs much more quickly than can be explained in terms of the forces discussed previously that naturally produce upward pressures on overhead.

The problem can be easily understood if one looks at the situation from the individual department's point of view. Each department believes its every action is truly needed. Each department feels it is at or exceeding its capacity level. Overhead budget cuts communicate that each department is expected to do the same volume of work with fewer people. (No one said anything else did they?)

In this approach any real reductions in service are left to the individual organizational units to sort out. This is very difficult to do informally because:

- The services are a complex "web" of transactions between multiple organizations (e.g., many organizations getting the same report) and no one or two organizations can see the whole picture.
- The individual organizations, because they have a narrow view of the value of what they produce don't believe that much of what they do can be safely eliminated.

The net result is a general lowering of service levels across the company and a gradual buildup of service-related problems. These problems become the reason to increase costs. "Snap back" has begun.

---

[4] Management almost never plans on actually achieving its full percentage target but perhaps 60 to 75% of it due to "give-backs" where they are required.

WHAT IT TAKES TO MANAGE OVERHEAD PROPERLY

The bad news is, there is no way to manage overhead costs without understanding each cost center's services both for internal units and the outside world and the value of these activities to the corporation. The good news is, an effort to understand these relationships and their value to the corporation will return the cost involved more efficiently than any other investment the company can make. This return comes in two forms, both of which are significant:

- A major reduction in overhead expenses.
- A material increase in the benefits to the corporation of the remaining overhead expense. (It is worth remembering that almost all the "investments" in the off-balance-sheet assets pass through these accounts.)

In a manufacturing organization overhead is 50 to 80 percent of all expenses. In service industries, with few or no material costs, this percentage is even higher. Even small efficiency improvements in overhead management have an enormous effect on the company's bottom line. In a company earning 5 percent on sales and with 50 percent of its costs in overhead, a 10 percent decrease in overhead would almost double reported profits.[5]

Of greater significance is the effect on the company's long-term competitive position. Overhead workers are not only involved in the company's daily delivery of products and services, they also manage almost all of the "investment" activities as well. Better managing these people and the other overhead expenditures will not only improve daily operations but also affect everything from product development to em-

---

[5]
$1.000 Sales	$1.000
.475 Var. cost	.475
.525 Gross margin	.525
.475 Fixed Cost	.4275
$ .050 Profit	$ .0975

ployee recruiting to the quality of the company's sales organization.

In order to manage overhead expense properly, management must do four things:

- Understand the maximum level of overhead that the company can afford on a *long-term* basis.
- Understand what the various cost center outputs are producing and the value of those outputs to the company.
- Adjust the overhead spending structure in terms of the type and volume of outputs; and adjust the methods used to produce them to the pattern that the company believes is in its best competitive interest.
- Create a management control system that manages the chosen pattern of outputs against overhead "creep" and that also allows the corporation to adjust its overhead spending as conditions change.

How Much Can Be Spent

Ask almost any manufacturing company manager about the company's direct labor or direct material cost and you will get an answer in terms of the level of these costs it can have for its various products and still be competitive. These same companies often have no idea of how much overhead can be carried and still earn a competitive return. A similar situation exists in service companies. Overhead expense is often viewed as "just there" and needing to be covered with an adequate volume of sales.

In fact, just as in the case of direct labor and material costs, the market is only prepared to support a given level of overhead expense. A company can cover this amount with a "normal" gross margin percentage and volume of sales and still have an adequate average return, over time. *Companies must be precise about what this level of overhead is,* not only because they wish to earn an adequate return, but because an adequate return is the *least* they can afford to earn and not experience problems in the longer run.

Failing to manage total overhead to a level that can be supported, in the hopes that sales and/or margins will increase to support a higher level, is similar to saying that product prices must be increased because direct labor or direct material costs are not competitive. The market simply will not pay for more overhead than the company's gross margin can support.

The gross margin is not going to increase because a company needs it to. In fact, a company's margins reflect its competitive position in its industry and typically change slowly following the company's competitive position. This is often obscured by the accounting system that reports large fluctuations in margins as sales change. If one measures the difference between sales and outside purchases less direct labor and other variable expense (i.e., true variable cost), margins are more stable. Margins change slowly as prices improve or decline with business conditions or as productivity changes. It is this average margin over the business cycle, plus a reasonable profit, that overhead expense must not exceed.

Knowing How Overhead is Spent in Terms of Outputs Produced

The second element in successfully managing overhead is understanding how it is actually used within the company. This involves understanding what outputs each cost center produces and for whom. These outputs have to be understood in terms of their cost and the value they have to the various organizations that use them. This can be complicated when several cost centers are involved in the production of a single output, such as a report, and likewise several cost centers may make use of it.

It is very important to think in terms of outputs produced and their value and not to focus on the activities that produce the outputs. Only the outputs have value to the user and, therefore, benefit the corporation. While this process is a time-consuming and expensive activity, it is at the heart of the process. Also, this step has to be done only infrequently if a continuing management program is successfully implemented.

Adjust the Pattern of Outputs and Producers

Armed with the knowledge of what is actually being produced, at what cost, and to what value, it is then possible to alter what is being done, and how it is done to increase the efficiency of the whole process. It is almost inevitable that there will be plenty of opportunities to do this for several reasons:

- Cost centers are rarely in a position to know the value of their outputs to the people who use them, let alone to evaluate their value from an overall corporate perspective.
- Users of outputs rarely are in a position to know the costs they are causing.
- The need, from an overall company viewpoint, for various overhead outputs changes over time. There is a tendency to add the new or changed requirements but to continue to produce those outputs that have become less valuable or even useless.
- The methodology for producing the outputs that remain can often be improved, once *a company understands* how they are produced (often by several cost centers) and understand their true cost.

When first done, this process of adjustment can generate an almost unbelievable number of cost-reduction opportunities. Probably two-thirds or more will come from eliminating or modifying outputs that are not worthwhile when their true costs and value are known. The remaining reductions will probably come from improvements in the way in which the various outputs are produced or the company is organized to produce them.

It is important to recognize that these improved methods do not include a presumption of a speedup. Speedups that are the result of a special study rarely "stick." To the extent that the work pace in an area is inadequate, the problem should be handled separately from a total review of overhead costs.

Understanding and evaluating a company's overhead costs through this approach can be very powerful, if properly executed. It is very important throughout this process that a company be prepared to deal with the large surplus personnel that can be a result. This approach, based on eliminating work and improving the methodology for doing the remaining functions, avoids the major reason for "snap back" inherent in the across-the-board approach. However, handling the surplus personnel improperly can also create snap back as they create "busy work." More importantly, not handling these people properly can have a devastating impact on management's credibility.

Creating a Continuing Overhead-Management System

The first step in improving a company's ability to control its overhead on an ongoing basis is to have control reporting be technically correct as described in the last chapter. As suggested in the beginning of this chapter, the main reason the current management system cannot effectively manage overhead costs is that we use budgets that are time-based and therefore are merely limits on inputs. There is no connection between the allowable expense and the level of output which needs to be produced. As described in Chapter 7, many of these costs can be controlled against output-related flexible budgets instead. Additionally, many costs are charged to cost centers which, in fact, do not control the costs. Correcting these problems is something every company can do with a minimum of disruption and expense.

However, this still leaves a good deal of expense in accounts that have time-based fixed budgets. The problem with this approach is the lack of knowledge by both producer and user of the cost effectiveness of the expenditures. One answer to this on a routine basis is to increase the company's use of the horizontal management techniques more fully described in Chapter 11.

As executives and employees better understand how overhead services are delivered and what their value is to the various organizations throughout the company, much of the mystery surrounding the use of overhead expense will disappear. Personal relationships should develop which will make mutual action in the interest of the overall company much easier.

It is not necessary for an individual functional department to wait for the corporation to devise horizontal management policies. Horizontal management can occur within a functional organization as well as between functional units. The major functional organizations—Sales, Operations, Engineering and Finance—consume a great deal of their own overhead expense. Because they have it within their control to practice horizontal management within themselves, they can manage overhead directly, no matter how they are managed by the corporation.

No matter how well the company has organized its overhead expenditures at any given time, it must be able to adjust expenditures as conditions change. There are not only the changes in the external world of competitive business, but also internal changes as well. The external world changes due to changes in customers' needs, actions of competitors, changes in the regulatory environment, and so forth. Internally, people come and go, the effectiveness of organizations changes, and the company learns to improve overall operations. The natural tendency of most companies is to add or modify overhead products and services to accommodate these changes. *It is very important to recognize that the need to accommodate change does not mean that overhead expenditures must increase.*

An organization practicing good horizontal management techniques and recognizing a fixed limit on its overhead expenditures should be able to accommodate change routinely. To the extent that increased expenditures are needed because the company is growing, the flexible budgets should supply the additional money that is required by the activities that are volume sensitive.

A good technique for monitoring the growth of overhead expense is to designate each account in each cost center as being one of the following:

- Variable.
- Volume-insensitive but discretionary.
- Truly fixed.

Variable expenses are those that are controlled with flexible budgets. Presumably, we are controlling these expenses to outputs produced using an agreed-upon methodology. The volume-insensitive but discretionary expenses are those expenses that management has decided to have that do not vary with the volume of sales or production. I favor calling these expenses "Programmed Expenses." A truly fixed expense is that expense which is not reachable by management within a budget cycle in a cost-effective way, for example property or equipment leases.

The company should then focus on the programmed-expense accounts. One way to do this is to divide programmed expense into:

- Those costs that are absolutely necessary to corporate survival and those expenditures that are made so the corporation can run better (the "nonessential" costs can then be examined each year to see if they are still appropriate).
- Those costs that serve customer needs directly and those that service internal needs (examine the internal services to see if they are cost-effective when viewed from the perspective of overall corporate profitability).

It is impossible to be a world-class competitor and manage overhead as if it were some "black hole" that cannot be managed in detail but must be managed in its totality. Overhead is not only the company's largest expense, it is also the path through which almost all of the investments in the company's off-balance-sheet assets are made.

Financial management as we use it does not and cannot do this job. It is necessary for management to make the effort to get into the details of these activities and actually manage what is going on. Our failure to do this is a primary reason many American companies are uncompetitive.

CHAPTER 9

SEIZING THE OPPORTUNITY TO BETTER MANAGE SERVICE

All companies sell their products "wrapped" in services. This is true of companies selling products that they manufacture, companies selling tangible products manufactured by others (such as retailers), or companies selling intangible (service) products such as banks and insurance companies.

Manufacturers wrap their products in technical instructions, delivery services, after-purchase services such as guarantees and repairs, and sometimes financial services. Retailers wrap their products in services such as store locations, selling floor services, and financing. Banks wrap their demand deposit, auto loan, and mortgage products in services such as branch hours of opening, teller services, and island services.

For most companies, improving the character and quality of the various service "wrappers" is *one of their best, if not the best,* short-run competitive opportunity. *However, most of management's attention and essentially all of the analogue management process focuses on the products themselves.*

While it is obviously important that a company strive to have the best products possible, products themselves are frequently not a good basis for building a competitive advantage. The reason is very simple. *Products have become very difficult to differentiate.* Manufacturing product technology is easily transported not only between companies but across national boundaries. The Japanese have proven that even the most sophisticated technology, such as electronic chips, can be copied and improved. Very good VCRs are built in Korea, a country that had virtually no electronic manufacturing capability a few years ago.

Service products, if anything, are even more difficult to differentiate. Most service company products can be easily matched by an able competitor. Virtually anyone can purchase a car and rent it out. Banking and insurance products are easily copied. Even airline seats that carry one to far-off destinations have proven to be easy to supply.

On the surface, the service wrappers for these products may not seem like a very good basis for competition. What is so difficult about writing the technical instructions for a product one already manufacturers? Or repairing it for that matter? Likewise, what is so difficult about renting cars or hotel rooms or servicing retail customers? In fact, manufacturers rarely use their best people in these "ancillary" activities. Service companies often use low-paid or even temporary employees to supply their service wrappers.

GOOD SERVICE IS HARD TO SUPPLY

In fact, it is difficult to supply good service, as every consumer knows. There are three fundamental reasons for this that make the process an open-ended, never-ending competitive opportunity:

- *Service cannot be inventoried.* It must be supplied on demand. Because most companies cannot exercise much control over when demand will occur and because the customer usually regards waiting as a reduction in service, solving this problem is a never-ending competitive opportunity.
- *Service is suppplied to individual human beings who experience the service in their own terms.* Unlike the

assembly line worker who services an inanimate object (say an automobile) as it passes, a bank teller or a retail clerk services an unending line of human customers. So does the customer service organization of a manufacturing company. These customers are different not only as human beings but also different in their needs for service at a particular moment. A first-time customer at a car rental counter needs different service than a regular customer at that same counter. A vehicle repair shop that has a customer whose car can't be driven has a different need for a part than one that is ordering that same part for its inventory.

- *Service can take the form of a bewildering number of hard-to-anticipate transactions.* Unlike the manufacturing worker who makes few real decisions about what to do each day, the worker who supplies service is routinely confronted by a variety of possibilities. A retail clerk may be asked any number of questions about merchandise, record several different types of transactions on her point-of-sale terminal, and deal with a lost child all in the same hour. The service suppliers in manufacturing companies or their contractors face innumerable, delivery and service "exceptions" each day.

THE SERVICE WRAPPER IS USUALLY UNDERMANAGED

In spite of the inherent difficulty of delivering a good service wrapper, most companies undermanage this area. The level of complaint about poor service provided by American companies is the most obvious evidence of this oversight. However, even if one didn't know this, one could tell that service was probably poor by looking at the processes most companies use to manage their service wrapper.

Many American companies have positioned their manufactured and services products versus their competitors' products very carefully. Manufacturers and service companies alike can describe how their cars, machine tools, checking accounts, and insurance policies stack up relative to similar products of their competitors. Companies frequently have specific plans for changing products and services based solely on a competitor's actions in the same market. How many of these same companies know how their service wrapper is positioned in the market place? Are they trying to be better than the competitor? Just as good? By when? How?

Besides not positioning their service wrappers in the marketplace, most companies have few, if any, management reports through which they can monitor actual performance. How many retailers can identify selling floor service targets and how they are performing against them? How many banks monitor the level of customer satisfaction with their branch services? How many manufacturing companies monitor the quality of their after-purchase repair services?

To the extent delivering the service wrapper is managed, the system is biased away from supplying good service. The most obvious formal management controls around the service wrapper in most companies are:

- Budgets.
- Procedures that must be followed by the employees of the company.
- Rules and procedures with which the customer must comply.

All of these management controls are intended to control the amount and type of input the company puts into the customer service activity, not how much satisfaction the customer gets.

The budgets restrict the amount of resources available no matter what happens. The procedures require an employee to follow a planned pattern of behavior, no matter what he or she learns about the situation. Customer rules exist to keep the customer from cheating the company or the company from doing things it wants the customers to do for themselves.

Once again we are relying on analogue management. The budget is merely a dollar *representation* of the level of human effort the company believes is adequate to deliver the service. The procedure is a *representation* of what *activities* the corporation *thinks* constitute good service. Likewise the customer procedures and rules are representations of what the corporation thinks is fair.

These approaches are borrowed from the technique the company uses to manage internal operations. When managing the manufacturing of its products or the doing of its accounting the company is dealing with problems that are inherently much simpler. The three conditions that make supplying service to the outside world difficult are greatly reduced.

1. Service can not be inventoried.
2. Service is supplied to individual human beings.
3. Service can involve a bewildering number of hard-to-anticipate transactions.

When manufacturing products, the three conditions are practically eliminated. Production *is* scheduled. Because conditions are more controllable, a rigid procedure can work better. If procedures need to be modified, the reasons are obvious and the authority to do so is nearby. Furthermore, a product doesn't care if the same procedure is used to manufacture it over and over again.

Even so, unlike when it is supplying services, the company still monitors performance like a hawk. Most manufacturing operations have daily reports that show performance against direct labor and direct material standards. Variances are *expected* and explained: broken tool, operator error, bad material, and so forth. Likewise with production schedules; if a product is troublesome to produce, the procedures are changed, often frequently, until one is found which will produce the desired result. After all of this, the product is still inspected to be sure things are continuing to go well.

Because they are inappropriate, *the use of rigid procedures, applied uniformly using a fixed budget, reduces the service wrappers' quality below that of the products themselves.* Service in most retail stores is worse in the minds of the customers than the products sold. Banks offer great products that you can hardly use because of long lines and uninformed employees. Many manufacturers offer good products, which customers like, but which are almost impossible to get repaired using their warranty systems, let alone when they are "out" of warranty.

HOW TO DELIVER BETTER SERVICE

The first step in improving a company's service wrapper is to define its basic components. Because the service wrapper has not been managed as such, and because this is another example of a horizontal management problem, this can take some doing.

In a manufacturing company, start with the customer and trace and define the customer's various relationships with the company. For example, the company could define a number of major categories such as product information or delivery services which would cover the types of services supplied. These could then be broken down into sub-services such as printed information to independent repair sources and so forth. As in the case of overhead services, many organizations can be involved in supplying even relatively small elements of the wrapper. For example, printed material may involve one or more engineering groups, a graphics organization, and the sales department.

A service company can follow a similar process. However, many *service companies will have a more complex task since service is their main product* (whether they admit it or not) and the relationships with their customers will usually be more complex. It is important to recognize that while the service company's products are wrapped in services, *these services are its main reason for being.* Managing the service wrapper is much more important for them than for most manufacturing companies.

After defining the service wrapper and identifying how it is delivered, *the next step is to determine the current level of service.* As the company gains insight into the elements of the service wrapper, which elements lend themselves to what sorts of measurement will begin to be apparent. It will probably not be possible to measure every element of service. Also it will probably be necessary to contact the customer directly to understand the following things:

- How he feels about the current level of service.
- The elements of the process he finds most valuable.
- What changes he would appreciate.

The company can now decide *how to position itself relative to its competitors*. While this decision can be made earlier, it is probably not meaningful to do so unless one understands the cost/benefit consequences of various positioning alternatives.

In positioning its service wrapper, the company is deciding how it wants its customers to compare its service wrapper to that of its competitors, both in what is offered and how it is delivered. The important words are *customer* and *competitors*. Service is what the customer believes it is, not what the company thinks it is. In most cases the customer can only think of this service in relative terms (i.e., relative to the company's competitors).

As part of the positioning activity a company can consider whether it wants to make use of a service guarantee; many companies such as Federal Express, Manpower Incorporated, Domino's Pizza and Caterpiller do. In an excellent article on the subject of service guarantees Christopher W. L. Hart[1] suggests a number of conditions, one or more of which can make the use of a service guarantee particularly powerful in the marketplace:

- The price is high.
- The customer's ego is on the line.
- The customer's expertise with the service is low.
- Negative consequences of service failure are high.

---

[1]Christopher W. L. Hart, "The Power of Unconditional Guarantees," Harvard Business Review (July–August 1988).

- The industry has a bad image for service quality.
- The company depends on frequent customer repurchases.
- The company's business is affected deeply by word of mouth.

It is useless and even counterproductive to plan to deliver better service than the company can deliver. It is also not necessary. As we shall see later, almost any company can improve its current service wrapper. Practically speaking, that is probably all the positioning flexibility that is needed at the beginning.

CREATING THE DELIVERY SYSTEM

Having understood the current service wrapper and having decided on the competitive position the company would like to occupy (i.e., best among competitors, average, etc.) the next step is to make those modifications to the delivery system that are required to attain the desired position.

Delivering good service is heavily dependent on organizational issues. Therefore, it can take some time to modify successfully a company's service wrapper. While the details are very company-specific, and are beyond the scope of this book, there are some general suggestions relative to designing improved service delivery systems which can be made.

First we will go back to the reasons why service is hard to deliver:

- Service can not be inventoried.
- Service is customer-specific.
- It is difficult to plan for all possible transactions.

Then the functional specifications of an ideal delivery system begin to emerge. Specifically, the system must deliver the envisioned service while simultaneously dealing with the three conditions that make this difficult.

Most service delivery systems are set up as if they were manufacturing processes. They are specified in great detail. Managers give many reasons for following the manufacturing pattern, which are quite legitimate in and of themselves:

- The desire to have employees use the "best" approach that can be devised from both a cost and service delivery point of view.
- The need to prompt inexperienced personnel through the service delivery process.
- The need to collect financial or inventory data.

Many managers would argue that their biggest problem in supplying services is that employees or customers won't use the procedures as they were intended to be used.

The problem with this rigid approach to supplying service is that it rests on an unspoken assumption, which is not true, that the facts of the individual service situation can be known ahead of time and a system designed to accommodate them. In fact, because of the three conditions, just the opposite is true. Almost nothing is known with surety ahead of time. We do not know:

- When or how much service will be required.
- What the individual customer needs will be from *his* perspective.
- What kind or number of transactions will need to be done.

It is then left to that person who supposedly needs so much direction to fit the customer requirements into our very rigid delivery system while simultaneously not losing the data, security, and other objectives the system was designed to accomplish. We have all experienced this as customers and have been frustrated by it. *This fundamental misunderstanding of the need for flexibility in the service delivery process is at the heart of America's bad service problem.*

An approach is required that helps the employee to understand the nature of the service delivery outcome the company is trying to achieve (i.e., we want the part delivered in 24 hours, we want the customer to believe our bank has the best service) and the nature of the company's need for data, security, and so forth. The formal delivery procedure should be presented to the employee as a method that will generally accomplish the desired outcome in a cost-effective way. The employees should be encouraged to use the system in a flexible fashion within circumstances as they find them.

Obviously, the better the employees can perform and the more inherent flexibility built into the delivery system, the better the service will be. Therefore, the management challenge occurs on both of these fronts. Companies that can attract, train, and motivate better personnel and implement the most cost-effective, flexible delivery systems will deliver the best service.

GOOD SERVICE NEED NOT BE MORE EXPENSIVE

Why should doing something better make it more expensive? The real cost of a service wrapper is the cost spent on service delivery *plus* the cost of service failures. To a manager used to seeing service handled poorly by low-paid, unmotivated employees this flexible approach to improving service delivery will probably seem hopelessly expensive. This is because the manager overlooks the hidden cost of service nondelivery.

It is true that supplying a higher level of service perfectly is, in general, more expensive than supplying a lower level of service just as perfectly. *However, supplying the same level of service more perfectly is not more expensive.* It is probably cheaper, in fact, as American manufacturing companies have discovered. Quality can be less expensive because one does not have the expense generated by inefficient delivery followed by the expense of dealing with service failures. A simple test of this proposition is to observe service delivery personnel and understand the incredible percentage of their time spent on making and correcting errors and helping customers who are trying to get errors resolved.

When the company positions its service wrapper against competition it is defining the level of service it is willing to pay for. The cost of the service wrapper is a function of *both* the level of service chosen and the quality with which the chosen level is actually delivered.

A SERVICE WRAPPER IMPROVEMENT STRATEGY IS INHERENTLY CONSERVATIVE AND HIGHLY LEVERAGED

Competing with the company's service wrapper is conservative. Developing new products is both expensive and risky. Improving the company's service wrapper is not. In fact, as we have seen, it could very well be self-funding under the "Quality-is-free" concept.

If the strategy fails it does so softly. If a company fails to attain a targeted level of service, it is unlikely that service or cost will actually become worse as a result of the effort. More likely the company has learned something about its organization that will help it change over time while simultaneously making some progress toward its targeted revised wrapper.

If the strategy succeeds it can be highly leveraged on the bottom line. Customers should be willing to pay more for the same product if a company's service wrapper is perceived to be better. Improving quality at any specific level of service is virtually without cost, thus an increase in revenue would fall directly to the bottom line. Because companies usually earn less than 10 percent on sales, even small changes in prices can produce very large increases in profits.

Improving the service wrapper, if successful, can be a source of a long-term competitive advantage. Improving the company's service wrapper can be more easily hidden from competitors than new or improved products. Furthermore, because it involves organizational behavioral change, a competitor cannot respond instantly. As a result, if the company is successful it gains lead time. Furthermore, the nature of the challenges presented by the three conditions which make supplying service difficult present a continuous competitive opportunity. A company only has to maintain its lead.

The nature of a customer's perceptions of the service wrapper is also helpful in this regard. Since customers cannot experience the competitor's service wrapper without using it, it is difficult for the competitor to change his reputation. To do so he may have to get ahead and stay ahead for some time, drawing equal will not usually get the job done.

In conclusion, this opportunity to compete using one's service wrapper may be the most neglected corporate "strategy" in American business. A company's reputation in this area is a major off-balance sheet asset. For service companies it may be their most important off-balance sheet asset.

The connection to our focus on analogue management and its tendency to bias management attention away from off-balance sheet assets is obvious. It should also be obvious that as companies depart the analogue management trap, identifying and better managing the various service wrappers that they supply to their customers becomes a marvelous competitive opportunity. Competing this way can be especially effective when used against many foreign competitors because of the distance and cultural disadvantages.

CHAPTER 10

CONTINUOUS COMPETITIVE ADVANTAGE

The objective of all management activity is to attain and maintain a competitive advantage. Said another way, a natural consequence of a capitalistic system is to produce a surplus of supply. *The objective of management is to be sure that surplus belongs to the competition.*

Up to this point, we have focused on what might be called micromanagement techniques: such as internal management information, management of overhead, and management of customer service. This chapter addresses a company's overall competitive stance. Specifically, three issues will be discussed:

- The role of formal strategy.
- The role of the core business.
- The role of the company's organization.

ATTAINING A SUSTAINABLE COMPETITIVE ADVANTAGE—THE ROLE OF STRATEGY

For years, business literature has been full of commentary about how to build sustainable competitive advantage through strategy. Underlying most of this rhetoric was the unspoken assumption that all that stood between management and the attainment of an insuperable lead over their competition was some "strategy," which would leave their competitors at a semipermanent disadvantage.

For those who are unfamiliar with the theoretical work surrounding this area,[1] a brief description may be helpful at this point. Grossly simplified, corporate strategy can be defined as focusing a company's activities so as to maximize its competitive advantage. In choosing the best strategy, extensive studies are made of the industry and the company's position in that industry relative to its competitors. The following elements of industry structure have been used:

- Intensity of competitive rivalry.
- Bargaining power of supplies.
- Bargaining power of customers.
- Threat of new entrants.
- Threat of substitute products.

Having understood the industry structure and the company's position, there are three generic strategy options:

- Be the low-cost producer in the industry.
- Differentiate the company's product/service package so as to command a higher price.
- Focus on an industry segment within which one attempts one of the first two strategies—low cost in the target segment or differentiation in the target segment.

The study of industry characteristics and the company's market position supply the information necessary to make a proper selection. Further, there is an implication that the insight gained will also provide a method of implementing the strategy which would allow the company to be more successful competitively. For example, by taking advantage of its superior scale or access to raw materials in a way not previously exploited, a company might become the low-cost producer in the industry.

Until the 1970s and early 1980s, most companies were unfamiliar with this approach. Therefore, it seemed to many

---

[1]See for example Michael E. Porter's *Competitive Strategy* (New York: Free Press, 1980).

within the business community that an enormous opportunity must exist to develop strategies which would produce sustainable competitive advantages.

Many years, internal studies, and consulting projects later, many people are beginning to doubt whether it is possible to attain a competitive advantage directly through intellectual activity in the face of determined and flexible competitors. Being in this camp, I believe it is Pollyannaish to expect a strategy in and of itself to produce a sustainable, competitive advantage. It is like a football team expecting to conceptualize offensive plays that are unstoppable while ignoring everything else that must be accomplished on the playing field.

Advocates of this approach mistake the basically true notion that if you are not thinking about your business strategically, you probably should, with the conclusion that if you did think strategically, something wonderful would happen. It is true that circumstances change and that some of these changes can present enormous competitive opportunity as well as risk. It is not true that just because a company stops to think, it will gain an enormous insight. *It is impossible to schedule insight,* particularly when the insights involve daily business activities. Competitors are perfectly capable of achieving the same results and, for the most part, have the same facts available. However, there are at least *two downside reasons* for a company to clarify its strategic position on a regular basis.

- Whether a strategic breakthrough is available or not, there is a need to have agreement on a company's strategy in order to focus management's behavior.
- An incorrect strategy can have enormous negative consequences.

The Need for Focus

At a minimum, a company needs to articulate its current strategy to be sure the current management team knows what the company's strategic stance is and is prepared to support it. Trying to do this can lead to a number of outcomes such as:

- No general agreement on the strategy.
- Agreement on what the company's strategy is, but many executives feeling it has not been properly thought through.
- Current strategy becoming at least potentially obsolete because the assumptions upon which it is based have changed or are changing.

Need Not to be "Wrong"

The company's strategy also has to be right enough to offer a viable course of action. To use one of Michael Porter's terms, some companies get "stuck in the middle." This means that it is not possible to classify their strategy into one of the generic categories mentioned earlier. When this occurs, the strategy is also certain to be worse than one that can be classified and is, therefore, wrong. Of course, it is also possible to choose a strategy that is in one of the generic categories but is wrong because of factual circumstances. *In either case, the company has a serious problem even when it effectively implements its strategy. Such companies will be below-average performers at best and could even fail completely.*

An example of a company "stuck in the middle" would be one that continues to compete across all the segments of an industry, but focuses its product development in only a few segments. It is "stuck in the middle" because it cannot decide whether it is a niche player or not.

Another example of an incorrect strategy would be if this same company then tried to be the low-cost producer in one or more of its market niches when its capability and reputation was for supplying high-quality products supported with good service. Becoming a low-cost producer would probably be impossible for this company because of the changes that would be required in the short run. It would be playing to its weakness instead of its strength. Knowing nothing else, it would seem far more rational for this company to try to be a differentiated niche player than a low-cost niche player.

The real purpose of strategic thinking is that it serve as a framework for rationally thinking about a company and as a means of focusing executives on the same competitive approach.

Being Right Is Not Enough

It is important not to confuse the considerable consequences of being wrong with the benefits of being right. Unfortunately, *but not unreasonably,* these consequences are not symmetrical. Being wrong is much more harmful than being right is beneficial. *Being right can be described as a necessary but not a sufficient condition for success.* The reason is very simple: *choosing a strategy does not make it happen.*

No matter how brilliant your strategy for doing so, choosing to be the low-cost producer in a market segment does not automatically achieve that goal. Even a "brilliant" strategy would have to be implemented and this could very well be difficult for a number of reasons:

- Many executives may not really understand the strategy or its potential.
- It may require more absolute change than is practically possible by the company's organization.
- It may seem to be a threat to operating results as reported by the accounting system, particularly in the short run.
- It may seem (or even be) very risky, even when viewed from a longer-range perspective.

Actually, it is very difficult to do anything well in a competitive business situation, let alone accomplish a significant change. It was the failure to understand this point that misled the business intellectual community, and some management consultants into believing strategic choice had more up-side potential than has thus far been demonstrated. The essence of the competitive problem is *being able to achieve organizationally those things that the company wishes.* However, before we focus on this critical issue, it is worthwhile to cover one other strategic issue, the role of the "core" business in the longer-term competitive process.

ATTAINING A SUSTAINABLE COMPETITIVE ADVANTAGE—THE ROLE OF THE CORE BUSINESS

Michael Porter uses the term *competitive strategy* to mean the strategies of the individual business units of a corporation and the term *corporate strategy* to describe the strategy the corporation uses as it attempts to attain synergy between its various business units. The previous comments in this chapter apply equally well to both types of strategies. However, there is an element of corporate strategy that is paramount, namely the role of the corporation's mainline or "core" business in this process. The failure to understand this role underlies a great number of problems American companies have with their corporate strategies. Said simply, a company has no choice about being successful in its core or mainline business for one simple reason: *a company cannot successfully leave its core business and continue to be a good investment for its stockholders*. If a board of directors concludes a company cannot be successful in its core business, it has only two choices:

- Try another management team.
- Sell the entire business—the core and any other business units.

Any other decision diminishes stockholder value.

This is not to say that a company that is successful in its core business, and is committed to remaining successful, cannot diversify itself to some degree. However, diversification cannot be a *substitute* for success in the mainline business and still preserve stockholder value. To think otherwise forces us to believe that the lack of success in the mainline business is completely beyond the control of management. It also assumes that the same management can buy and successfully manage other businesses, with which they are less familiar, better than the current management of those other businesses can.

In rare cases, management that is successful in its core business may choose to create another core business gradually. If the management is truly exceptional, it may be able to accomplish this goal without reducing shareholder value. However, since shareholders can diversify themselves, this objective is a difficult one to achieve.

The central issue here however, is not the possibility of diversification, but rather the need to be successful in the core business. A number of American companies have and are still turning away from their core business in subtle and not so subtle ways. These companies can be classified into two basic categories.

- Those that run from their mainline business.
- Those that engage in portfolio management.

Both groups are characterized by the fact that management reduces its focus on running the mainline business. In the first case, management usually declares that the mainline business has a limited future and that it is thus necessary for the corporation to concentrate on more promising lines of business if it is to produce an above average return for its shareholders. This will be accomplished, so the general story goes, by investing the cash flow from the mainline business in the more promising business units that the company already owns. If the corporation does not have a sufficient stock of these better investment opportunities, which is frequently the case, the company's stock and cash flow (to support debt) will be used to acquire them.

In the case of portfolio management, the company's mainline business is usually successful but, in the opinion of management, unable to properly use its cash flow or the skills of the management team. Therefore, management creates a holding company arrangement within which a "portfolio" of companies or groups of companies will be held. The former mainline business is one of these holdings.

Each of the business units in the portfolio is managed in a decentralized fashion. The job of corporate management is to:

- Supply corporate oversight to the various operations.
- Shift cash flows between the members of the portfolio to maximize corporate return.
- Add and subtract companies in the portfolio.

The Results Have Not Been Good

The results of both of these ways of deemphasizing the core business have proven to be remarkably unsuccessful over the years. Further, many of the companies that have had problems as a result of "abandoning" their main business have announced they are returning to a policy of emphasizing it. This seems to be generally true whether the main business was originally judged to have a good future or not.

But why should this be? Why should something that has been done by so many companies with apparently sophisticated management turn out so badly? Why is it next to impossible to successfully abandon the mainline business? To understand this, it is probably worth a brief look at the logic which underlies much of this behavior. The logic comes from the same strategic management concepts that came to the fore during the middle and late 1970s. Oversimplified somewhat, it goes as follows:

- It is not possible to do well, (defined as continued increased sales and profits) in low-growth industries.
- Therefore, the cash flow generated by a good performer in a low-growth industry is better invested in a higher-growth industry rather than returning "surplus" cash to the stockholders.
- If a company has a diversified group of business units, they should be divided into cash generators (sometimes called "cash cows") and cash users based on the attractiveness of the industries in which they compete and, to some degree, the competitive position of the corporate "entry" in that market.

- To the extent that a company does not have enough cash users or, if the ones it does have are not placed well competitively, more business units should be acquired.
- Which business units were suppliers versus users of cash should be, in some cases, even announced publicly.

In many cases, the cash suppliers that were identified were the core business of the corporation. This is not too surprising when one considers that, particularly in large corporations, the core business tends to be in older, more "mature" industries with inherently lower growth rates.[2] (Especially when growth rates are expressed in percentage rather than absolute terms.) This logic is based on two unspoken assumptions:

- The "cash cows" will continue to be at least as success-ful as they are.
- The cash invested in the "more promising" business units will have a higher return than would the same cash had it been invested in the "cash cows" or returned to the stockholders.

In fact, in an amazing number of cases, both of these assumptions have turned out not to be true. This is especially true when the core businesses have been named "cash cows." The reasons for failure, in my opinion, are very obvious.

Let's take the first assumption, that the cash cow will continue to be successful. Naming a business as a "cash cow" has a devastating effect on it competitively. Consider these things:

- We have just told the management team and current and potential employees that the business unit has a much-diminished future.
- We have told our customers we no longer consider the business unit that supplies them to be as important to

---

[2]Companies in which this was not true were not tempted to use their core business as cash cows and are not relevant to this discussion.

us as it has been. (Maybe we will even sell it sometime in the future.)
- We have told the competitors of that business unit we will no longer make high-risk investments to improve its competitive position.

One could go on, but the point is obvious. *It is very hard to compete half-heartedly and successfully at the same time.* After all, the day before it was named a "cash cow" the management of the business unit in question thought it was competing flat out and that it could profitably use all the cash it could keep from the stockholders. (And it probably had a list of unfunded capital projects to support its contention.) In my view, one would be quite justified in asking why any responsible management would take the risk of naming its core business a "cash cow."

This problem does not stop with the first unspoken assumption. The second assumption, that higher return investments can be made in the cash-using business units, has turned out to be false in a surprising number of cases as well. Not only have the earnings been disappointing, but a number of other mistakes have been made as well, from force-feeding units in an attempt to have them grow faster than they could (cash is rarely, if ever, the only restraint on growth), to acquiring companies at dubious prices because they were needed to implement the corporate strategy. Many of these mistakes come from the fact that management did not understand the other businesses as well as the core business and certainly did not have a track record of successfully growing such businesses.

The important point is that all of this occurred at some cost to the core business, thus weakening it. The net effect is often a corporation that is competitively weaker, consisting of a weaker core business and a number of other business units, many of which are performing poorly.

However, *being dedicated to success in the core business obviously does not, in and of itself, produce a sustainable competitive advantage.* In fact, one might argue that, like avoiding other strategic errors, all one has accomplished with the realization that a company must be successful in its core business, is to avoid a very serious mistake.

SUSTAINABLE COMPETITIVE ADVANTAGE— THE ROLE OF THE ORGANIZATION IS PARAMOUNT

How then does one attain this elusive "Sustainable Competitive Advantage"? Is it even possible, except by accident or in special circumstances? Successful selection of a proper competitive strategy plays the limited role of not making it impossible. Further, a willingness to change the strategic focus as circumstances change is also important, as is the need to focus on success in the "core business."

However, whatever strategic approach is selected, the game will still degenerate into a head-to-head competition among competitors using that same general strategy. Further, there is also a potential for head-to-head competition with companies using other strategies, particularly with those who may be "stuck in the middle." This is the essence of the implementation problem described earlier in this chapter.

One could use the analogy of an athletic competition, say American football. Each team in the league has carefully chosen an overall strategy that it feels is its best approach. Some teams will emphasize defense, others offense. Within these broad categories, some offensive teams will be primarily running, ball-control teams. Others will be "big-play" teams and so forth. To win games and, ultimately, more than an average number of games, a team must not only execute its strategy but also execute it well enough to beat the other teams that know its strategy and are doing their best to frustrate its implementation. The same is true in business. A company cannot be above average if it cannot dominate some if not all of its competitors. Good strategy helps. An absence of bad strategy is essential.

The real competition is not between strategies, but between organizations. Given that each business organization is in some position on any given day and that this place can be described by such things as market position, products, physical capital, etc., what can management actually do to improve the situation? Whatever it can and ultimately does do will have to be done by the individual managers and other people in the organization. Technological development is undertaken by people, markets are won by people, even capital is attracted by people. Certainly great strategic insights are had by people. *Since this is true, there is no more important business management objective than building an organization that works perfectly.*

Furthermore, *advantages gained in developing an organization are sustainable* because it takes time and a sustained effort to build a talented, coordinated, and committed organization. Because people and circumstances continually change, the job is never done. An ability to do this better than one's competitors offers a continuous competitive opportunity.

So where in the company's strategic statements and management's control systems is the evidence that corporate managers actually believe this and are trying to build their organizations? *In fact, building the organization is essentially an unmanaged activity in most companies.* Our current American management technology ignores the acquisition, development, and retention of people as a competitive management activity. To the extent it is managed at all, it is relegated to staff specialists.

In most companies, it is impossible to find objectives and tactics to support competitive success in this area. Neither are there management reports with performance targets. Senior managers pretty much take the quality of the organization and its fundamental ability to function as a given and see their job as getting the most out of what they are stuck with.

As a result, it is not easy to identify a body of knowledge and/or agreement on what good organizational development behavior is. Compared to courses in financial analysis, the business schools offer very few courses in this area. The business press essentially ignores the problem as well, preferring to focus on the feats of individual managers as they wring performances from their organizations rather than develop them.

Companies in general would deny this, pointing to their elaborate college recruiting programs and expensive human resources departments. But where are the top students a few years later and where is the star manager who became a star because he could build organizations that continued to be top performers over and over after he was promoted from them?

While there are indeed such managers (thank goodness!), our analogue-driven, control-oriented management system actually puts negative pressures on these executives by forcing them to develop organizations in spite of the measurement systems. Our management system frequently rewards executives equally, or better, who do just the opposite and leave a string of demoralized and diminished organizations behind them as they move up the corporate ladder.

ELEMENTS OF ORGANIZATION BUILDING

If it is really all about our people versus their people what are the characteristics of a company that is successful in this area? There are several:

- Organization building is a conscience objective of the company and everybody knows it.
- Organization building is recognized as a line management activity.
- Line managers are evaluated on how well they develop people and promote organizational cooperation.
- There is an understanding within the company of organizational development and how the company intends to accomplish it.
- Organizational development extends to the bottom of the organization.

Organization Building Is a Conscious Objective of the Company and Everybody Knows It

Companies that have developed superior organizations and have sustained them over the years, such as IBM, did it on purpose. They knew what they wanted to do and communicated this objective throughout the organization in a way that was believable. While many in senior management say things such as "people are our biggest asset" their actual behavior often does not support their claim and the rest of the company does not believe them. The most obvious case comes when something goes wrong and management must choose between preserving and continuing to build the organization and some other goal, such as short term profits—especially when executive bonuses are tied to them. People do understand senior management has to balance several objectives. The question is whether the organization gets its share.

The good news is that if organization building is really a top management objective, its normal actions in this direction will automatically signal the rest of the organization.

Organization Building Is Recognized as a Line-Management Activity

A staff-driven organization-development program is an oxymoron. If this sounds strange, it is probably another symptom of how far from reality our current management system has gotten us. Organizational development is a line activity simply because it must be. There is no other way to do it. *Over 90 percent of everything a person learns about his or her job, or feels about the organization, comes from his or her day in and day out contacts within the company.*

If the immediate supervisor is a good teacher and enthusiastic about the organization, this will be passed on. The same is true of the opposite. People who stay with an organization try to fit in. If the management group role models properly, the rest will take care of itself. If it doesn't, no amount of staff work or top management rhetoric will undo the damage.

Line Managers Are Evaluated on How Well They Develop People and Promote Organizational Cooperation

If organizational development is a line activity, it is naturally a part of the evaluation of a line manager. If this seems incompatible with the other measures of his performance, it probably says something negative about those other measures. All other things being equal, it should be obvious that good developers succeed faster than those who are not so good. Bad developers should not succeed at all because their other attainments are not really as valuable as they seem because they damage the company's most important competitive asset, its human organization.

There Is an Understanding within the Company of Organizational Development and How the Company Intends to Accomplish It

Given that a company means to emphasize organizational development and line managers know it is their responsibility, there is still the matter of developing and communicating what the technology of organizational development is—what we believe works and what doesn't. What is the manager's role and what is the subordinate's responsibility? How well this technology is worked out, communicated, and executed is the ultimate determination of how well the company develops and maintains its organization competitively. Some Japanese companies have brought this to a fine art which they seem to be able to employ cross-culturally (i.e., with non-Japanese workers and managers).

Organizational Development Extends to the Bottom of the Organization

Organizational development is *not* management development. Most of the real work in an organization is done by nonmanagers. Therefore, how well the company competes "on the field" is really a function of how well the nonmanagement personnel perform. Whether production workers, sales people, or billing clerks, these are the people who do the work that is seen in the marketplace and represents the company.

Thus the ultimate objective is to have the organization in a position where it can do the following:

- Attract anyone to it that it wants to hire.
- Keep anyone it wants to keep.
- Expect people to operate in the company's interest with insight and with enthusiasm.

This can only be accomplished when people see their own interest as being best served by being part of the company and helping to foster its success. *This is the ultimate objective of all organization-building activity.*

THE CONCEPT OF CONTINUOUS COMPETITIVE ADVANTAGE

Most people use "sustainable competitive advantage" to mean a competitive advantage that a company achieves *at a point in time.* This advantage then allows the company to continue to be an above-average, and possibly the dominant competitor in its industry for an indefinite period of time.

Instead, companies should pursue an overall competitive approach that focuses on the overwhelming role the human organization plays in the competitive process. Strategically, the human organization is the best competitive opportunity and the biggest limitation a company has. What is sought is a competitive advantage based on overwhelming the competition with the excellence of the company's day-to-day operations and with the execution of its macrostrategies. This can be thought of as focusing on developing and maintaining a *continuous competitive advantage* rather than attempting to bet everything (albeit unintentionally) on a "big win."

Continuous competitive advantage rejects the idea of semipermanent victories in the competitive battle and instead focuses on the need to win continuously in a battle that never ends. While it is clearly possible to get a "big win" competitively, our preoccupation with this approach diverts attention from the things companies must do to insure their longer-run competitive survival.

If this approach seems simplistic or, on the contrary, unmanageable, it is a tribute to the extent analogue management has removed managers from the real job of managing their companies. Why shouldn't the best organizations win? Why should inferior organizations do well?

Continuous competitive advantage is also the best way to *discover* and *implement* a major strategic opportunity if one exists, for several reasons:

- True business insights have as a necessary, if not sufficient, condition that the executives be close to the realities of the business. This approach produces executives who are.
- Better people have a better chance of having good insights. This approach aims to have better people.
- Organizations that function well together know and can do more than organizations that are not functioning well within and between their various areas.

Circumstances change and people themselves change over time, thus this approach requires a continual effort on the part of the company. The job is never done. This is, of course, good and bad news. The bad news is that any level of organizational perfection attained is, by definition, temporary. The good news is that it is possible to continue to improve almost indefinitely. *The best news is that this reality is true whether it is consciously recognized or not.*

The conventional thinking about attaining a sustainable competitive advantage seems to ignore the organization, particularly as a limitation to the strategic process with the following results:

- Proposed strategies cannot be and are not implemented because of organizational limitations.

- Proposed strategies unintentionally damage the organizational assets, such as when business units are declared "cash cows."
- Proposed strategies focus top management and much of the rest of the organization away from the job of pursuing excellence in the company's day-to-day operations.

Because essentially all companies are "people limited" (whether they know it or not), the strategy of *continuous competitive advantage* has the benefit of maximizing *real* internal growth, and this growth *will* be picked up by the accounting analogue. It also maximizes a company's ability to successfully acquire other companies. The usual reason acquisitions fail is that the executives of the acquired company cannot see any reason to stay, and if they do stay, any reason to be enthusiastic about the new management. Companies pursuing the concept of continuous competitive advantage should have two advantages in dealing with the problem:

- Good skills that they can use to preserve the human organization for which they have just paid so much.
- "Extra" human resources of their own to put in the acquired company should this be either desirable or necessary.

There really is such a thing as a sustainable competitive advantage after all! It just looks too simple (even though it isn't) to satisfy our analogue management mentality. In fact, it is analogue management that is simplistic because it leaves a company with no real *dependable* hope of attaining a sustainable competitive advantage.

CHAPTER 11

CORE COMPETITIVE POLICIES AND HORIZONTAL MANAGEMENT

This chapter builds on the idea that business competition is between the human organizations of the companies involved. It focuses on two questions:

- How can a company strengthen its organization? (Core policies)
- How can it manage the various organizational units within the company so that they will work better together? (Horizontal management)

As was suggested in Part I, our analogue-driven approach to management does a miserable job in both of these areas. In most companies the development of people is an almost unmanaged activity in the hands of staff specialists. Meanwhile, interorganizational cooperation is stifled by the performance-measuring systems we have discussed.

As a result, there is not much agreement on the American management scene about how to accomplish organizational improvement. This can be clearly seen if one looks at a business school curriculum or a sophisticated business management periodical. There will be much more financially oriented content than organizationally oriented content. Furthermore, the "human resource" and organizational ideas will not come from as well-established an orthodoxy as will the financial material.

The concepts in this chapter are presented under two headings:

- Core policies.
- Horizontal management.

CORE POLICIES

One can argue that a company is not only *limited* by its human organization, but that people are the only *manageable* resource as well. People manage the company's assets (on-or off-balance-sheet) and it is people who are affected by the management process. Managers manage the behavior of other managers and of employees.

We do not manage product design; we manage product designers. We do not manage sales; we manage salespeople and advertising agencies. The capital budgeting system with its "hurdle" rate and approval process is just a way of managing the behavior of people who buy equipment and make other capital investments. The production schedule in the plant and the closing schedule in the accounting department are just ways of managing the activities of workers and their managers as they do their jobs.

Because this is true, unlike the other off-balance-sheet assets such as market share or the product portfolio, *the human organization is involved in every management action.* Under it all, *this is the reason that the quality of a company's management process is sharply limited by the quality of the company's human organization.*

Also because this is true, the overwhelming influence on the organizational development process, and therefore the quality of this asset, is the way day in, day out business is carried on. That is why organizational development is a line management responsibility. It simply cannot be otherwise. There is no way to counteract effectively this overwhelming influence. *Therefore, what is needed is some way to "bake" the organizational development process into the normal manage-*

FIGURE 11-1

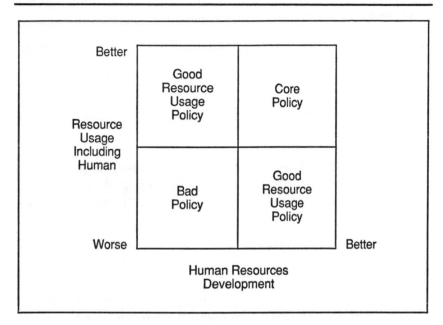

ment process. Obviously, the best way to do this would be to find corporate policies that are both good ways of managing the business and good for organizational development at the same time. I choose to call such a policy a "core" policy. Figure 11-1 is intended to illustrate this point.

In this diagram, a core policy is a policy that has the characteristics of being a good way of both deploying the company's resources[1] to create value and at the same time enhancing the company's human resources asset which is inseparably involved in the process. It also suggests that there can be policies that are good for resource usage but bad for the company's people assets and vice versa.

For a policy to be useful in enhancing the human resource asset, it would have to be the type of policy that would cause

---

[1]Human and nonhuman, on-balance-sheet and off-balance-sheet

executives and employees to change along one or more of the following dimensions.

- Becoming more *able to operate* in the company's interest.
- Becoming more *willing to operate* in the company's interest.
- Becoming more *willing to join or to remain* with the company.

Policies that diminish the asset would generally produce effects that are the opposite of the enhancing characteristics (e.g., making people less willing to operate in the company's interest).

To my knowledge, there is no "term of art" in the American management literature that describes the phenomenon I have called a core policy. So I have invented the term. However, the concept is hardly unknown. I would suggest that this is really the unifying concept beneath what has come to be called Japanese management. When the Japanese became successful competitors in our home market, we began to realize that they were using management techniques quite different than ours. At first we tended to downplay them as culturally driven. Subsequently, we have successfully copied a number of them.

Further in the United States and in Western cultures around the world, the Japanese have demonstrated that they can manage operations to standards approaching those they attain in Japan and do this using their normal management policies. Clearly, there is some universal truth underlying their approach to management or it would not copy and travel as well as it does. I would postulate this "truth" lies in their ability to better manage the company's human organization. Since the human organization is involved in everything else, the whole management process goes better.

Whether or not they are using the strategic approach of Continuous Competitive Advantage described in Chapter 10, I would leave to them to say. However, I believe it is quite obvious that they understand that companies compete through their organizations and that they very consciously do this. Furthermore, I believe they attempt to use what I have called "core policies" in this process and that their well-known group decision process is an illustration of such a policy. Simply stated, this policy says, "Get the input and agreement of all interested parties before a decision is made."

There are two risks with any decision:

- The decision is wrong and will result in a poor resource allocation.
- The decision is poorly implemented.

In the United States, we focus on the first risk and regard implementation as a foregone conclusion. The Japanese are just the opposite. They regard implementation as the risk. I remember the first time I heard a Japanese executive say this. My associates and I were helping Kawasaki Heavy Industries open its first American plant in the mid-1970s. I asked the Japanese manager what he thought of the then-prevalent accusation that Japanese managers' decisions were too slow, that they seem to talk them over among themselves forever. He smiled and said, "What would you say if I told you we thought American managers were slower?" I replied I would be surprised. He said, "In the opinion of many Japanese managers, American managers are quick to make decisions but slow to implement them. Japanese managers are slow to make a decision but by the time it is made it is almost implemented." He might have added "and with less risk of distortion."

This focus on implementation risk is a clear recognition of the role of people in the process. The seemingly endless discussion is an example of a core policy working its way out. Using our two dimensions in Figure 11-1, let's see what the basic assumptions behind it are.

On the better-resource-allocation axis they are attempting to achieve the following:

- A better basic decision through better input and more thoughtful consideration.

- Better implementation because the implementors: 1) Agree with the decision and are therefore more committed to its success, and 2) Understand why the decision was made and therefore understand what new problems or increase in old problems they can expect as they implement it.
- Better handling of unanticipated problems in the spirit in which the decision was made.

On the human-resource-development axis they are attempting to achieve:[2]

- More organizational insight into whatever subject of the decision, including how the decisions in this area impact other areas of the company.
- Development of the individual people involved in the decision discussions.
- A more enthusiastic commitment to the company and to cooperating with others in it.

Since all policies affect both axes of the diagram, the reason this policy qualifies as a core policy is that it accomplishes both the resource allocation and human resource development tasks *positively*. Any other decision-making policy that achieved the same ends would also be a core policy.

What makes this policy worth discussing here is that it seems to work. That is, the trade-off between speed, cost of decision making, and results seems to be well made. The fact that this process was and still is counterintuitive to many analogue managers is another reason. Before going into this issue more deeply, let us focus for a moment on the subject of horizontal management.

HORIZONTAL MANAGEMENT

All companies of any size are divided functionally into line and staff departments such as manufacturing, sales, engi-

---

[2]See the criteria for effective resource development discussed earlier in the chapter.

neering, legal, and so forth. Larger companies (and some not so large) may have divisions that are themselves divided functionally. This functional approach to organization is so universal that it is one of the few things all industries seem to have in common. Manufacturers, insurance companies, and retailers all recognize the need for functional specialization within their companies.

The reason for specialization is obvious. How can one be an accountant and an engineer at the same time? This same perceived need for technical expertise causes the formation of staff specialty groups such as public relations, when a company thinks it has enough need for the particular expertise to justify having an internal person or group. However, every solution creates a new set of problems—even a solution as universally used as functional specialization. The new problem is how to get these various organizational units to work together.

While the reason for the units needing to work together is obvious, it is worth stating. *The customer almost never experiences the functional organizations separately, he only sees them together.* However, good as it may be, the Ford Motor engineering organization is only experienced by the customer in the form of a car, which has been manufactured and sold by other parts of the organization. The same is true of any manufacturing organization, including those that produce industrial products. It is also true for service organizations. Whether the company is a retailer, a bank, or a car rental company, the customer only experiences the company as a whole. The customer making a purchase in a retail store is not conscious of the buying department or billing department as separate from store operations.

There are a number of naturally occurring reasons why the various functional organizations of a company should have trouble working together. These include such things as background and personality types of the people drawn to the various functional specialties, as well as the lack of understanding of the roles of other functional units inherent in this specialized organizational approach. Most managers seem to understand this fact.

One would think then that one finds within the management processes techniques that are focused on assuring cross-functional harmony. Professional football teams, for example, seem to understand this management problem very well. The players at the various positions have different jobs to do so that the team can be successful. On offense, for example, the interior linemen do a different job than the wide receivers, quarterback, or running backs. Football teams recognize the need for these different skills by having separate coaches for each of these positions. Each specialty coach teaches and drills his players on the techniques needed to play interior line, running back, and so forth.

No matter how intense this activity might get or how well one group may progress, none believes success in these individual activities constitutes a great offense. They recognize that all the functional specialties must perform together for that to be true. They also recognize that this frequently requires each group to do things which, when taken separately, will suboptimize their individual performance. During running plays some, if not all, wide receivers attempt to block. They do this even though blocking is not their best activity and doing so may tire or injure them and make them less able to run their pass patterns.

The players perform these suboptimal activities even though they are being individually graded by their specialty coaches from the game film for two reasons:

- There is a separate coach called (interestingly enough) an offensive coordinator who is responsible for the whole offense.
- There is an understanding on the part of their specialty coaches that cooperative behavior is necessary and they grade that as well.

In American business we do not seem to have the problem as well understood. We are very focused on the functional-excellence issue but we don't seem to recognize the need to encourage cross-functional cooperation, never mind requiring the need for it even at the expense of suboptimal functional performance. Many believe that there is nothing that can be done other than to *rely on internal competition to balance matters in the company's best interest.*

Yet the changes being copied from the Japanese are frequently improvements in horizontal management. For example:

- *Just In Time* (JIT) is a recognition that inventories are a cost of buffering the lack of communication and cooperation between companies and their suppliers or between departments within the company.
- Designing for manufacturability is nothing more than increasing the cooperation between product designers (engineering) and those who must make the product (manufacturing).
- Reducing the number of job classifications in a factory, in order to be able to move workers between jobs and departments as the situation requires, is horizontal management within the structure of the factory.

MANAGING THESE UNIVERSAL TRUTHS

What we have then is a need to manage two universal truths:

- The quality of the company's human organization is inextricably tied to the way in which the day in, day out line management activity is carried out.
- The company's success in serving its customers is a function of *overall* company performance, not the performance of the individual functional entities.

The bad news is whatever management does, there is nothing it can do to change these realities. Instead it must manage in their presence. The good news is that *managing in the presence of* these realities may be the best long-run opportunity most senior management teams have. *They can seize this opportunity through the creation and enforcement of "core policies."*

Luckily, the nature of core policies makes them the very kinds of things a top manager can "reach" and cause to occur. They are the ideal way to really influence the quality with which the daily activities of the company are carried out, while at the same time building organizational strength for the future. What greater security can a company have than the assurances that it can dominate its competitors "head to head" through the superiority of its own people and their ability to cooperate in the company's best interest. The reason this opportunity exists is that the control-oriented, analogue-driven management process used in most American companies not only ignores the management of these realities but actually is counterproductive to both development and cooperation.

What we are trying to create are the opposites of the organizational characteristics discussed in Chapter 3. We want an organization which is:

- Not receiving micro direction from its top management.
- Focused on developing all the firm's assets, whether on or off the balance sheet.
- Internally cooperative both within and between the various organizational units.
- Nimble.
- Outward looking.

Further, we want a management process that minimizes for the individual managers (and employees for that matter) the problems listed in Chapter 3 and instead makes people more willing and more able to function in the company's interest.

SOME CORE POLICIES

So what would core policies that promote individual development and better deploy all the firms resources look like? (While better deployment does not automatically mean better horizontal management, but as we shall see, it frequently does.)

The list is limited only by the company's commitment to organizational development and the skill of top management in this area, five policies will be discussed here. If properly executed, the following *could* become core policies:

- Evaluate and promote line managers on the basis of their people development and interorganizational skills and accomplishments as well as for how well they do the rest of their job.
- Transfer managers and, potentially, employees between functional departments, within functional departments and between line and staff jobs for horizontal management and personal development reasons. Consider internal transfers for executives who may have peaked.
- "Unhook" compensation from the need to occupy a position, be promoted, or manage a larger organization.
- Consciously limit the number of middle management and staff jobs.
- Do not "hard wire" compensation to analogue goals, not even overall company profits.

In order for these policies to be true core policies, they must promote individual and organizational development and enhance the quality of the management process itself. Each of these suggested policies has the potential to do this if properly implemented. Let us see how.

Evaluate Managers on Human Resource Development and Interorganization Cooperation

If the first of our "truths" is in fact true, then a person's experience in doing his or her line job completely overwhelms any other development activity that he or she might experience. Therefore senior management must explain to itself what it is doing to manage this development so it will occur (and it will occur) in a way that is in the company's interest. The most direct way to do this is to put human resources development into the normal line management evaluation process.

The normal analogue evaluation process not only is unable to measure this development activity but it may actually be counterproductive to it. There is no way to tell if the responsible executive is destroying or enhancing the company's human resources he manages.

This policy says that management will consciously try to determine this over time and evaluate the executives accordingly. If done properly, this policy will result in better evaluations for those executives who develop the people entrusted to them than for those executives who do not develop people (even destroy them) but who otherwise perform equally well.

For this policy to be a successful core policy one question still remains. On average, will executives who are better "people developers" get the same or more performance out of their people than those executives who are not? If we return to the three criteria for successful development, which are:

- People are more able to contribute.
- People are more willing to contribute.
- People are more willing to join and stay.

It would seem that better developers should be able to get more performance from their employees. (Obviously if they only get as much, the company would still be better off). Further, since this development occurs as a normal part of the line activity, there is no obvious "cost" associated with it as there would be if the employees were removed from their normal work for training.

Transfer Managers (and Potentially Others) for Horizontal Management and Developmental Reasons

Japanese companies and some American companies have found that by transferring people between organizational units, familiarity and a resulting rapport can be established. However, when managers are focused on their own performance as reported by an analogue and little else, they are reluctant to "give up" a capable employee and in some cases reluctant to receive one who is unfamiliar with the work of their organization.

The fact is that this internal transfer policy has the potential for being a very powerful core policy. The effect on the organization of having executives with a broader understanding of the company can completely overwhelm any temporary loss of efficiency the transfers may cause. The benefit occurs both in the executive's ability to do his own job better in the overall interest of the company and also in his improved ability to participate in the horizontal management process.

This transfer of managers policy suggestion would be counterintuitive to most American managers. The rule in most American companies is that a person never transfers from his functional department. In many companies, particularly large ones, the rule is defined much more narrowly than that, often confining a person to a very narrow promotional path. This policy of not transferring people results in two very negative outcomes:

- Valuable managers leave for lack of perceived opportunity.
- There is often a very high level of mistrust, sometimes bordering on hostility, between organization units whose job is to cooperate with each other.

On the latter point, people seem prepared to believe more negative things about other organizations in their companies than they would believe about other people when outside of their work experience. For example, that people in other departments would deliberately and repeatedly do things to frustrate them for no apparent reason.

This loss of resources, underutilization of resources, and pressure on the horizontal management process are to a large degree an outgrowth of the analogue management process which tends to focus each organizational unit on itself and fails to focus on managing human resources development and horizontal management as part of managing the line activities. This transfer policy suggestion is intended to work on both of these problems. Experience suggests that once people know one another and understand each other's problems, ways can be developed to solve problems they may have had in cooperating.

However, some would say that the internal transfer policy accomplishes these things at the expense of functional organizational focus and control. Clearly some balance must be maintained. However, our present approach clearly over-balances in the direction of functional focus and largely ignores the people development and horizontal management problems. As far as I know, the best discussion of this problem of the need for functional focus versus interfunctional cooperation is *Organization and Environment* by Paul R. Lawrence and Jay W. Lorsch. I would particularly recommend the first three chapters of this excellent book for an overview of this problem.

Unhook Compensation

Currently, compensation in most American companies is tied to a person's position and to the characteristics of that position rather than to the person himself. The effect of this is often to put people in the wrong jobs so that they can be compensated. It also causes managers to do things like trying to increase the number of people in their organizations whether this is in the company's interest or not.

This is a classic case of doing the wrong thing for the right reason, especially in organizations, such as engineering and sales, where a person's ability to contribute as an individual is important. What often happens is a person is "promoted" to a management job so that he can be compensated even though he has little ability for, or interest in, management. (This approach to compensation is also one of the reasons American companies have so many middle management jobs.)

There is no direct business imperative that requires us to pay people in this fashion. It is again a result of our fascination with analogues as a way of managing things. In this case, the analogue is a position description or a point system that establishes a salary range, no matter who is in that position.

For this policy to be a successful core policy, a company must find a fair way to compensate people that allow them to function in a position that maximizes their contribution to the company and promotes their own personal growth and their ability to foster the growth of others. Successfully doing this would accomplish our goal for a core policy of simultaneously promoting the growth of the company's human resources and maximizing the deployment of these and the company's other resources.

Limit the Number of Middle Management and Staff Jobs

The effect on the American management process *and the reasons for* our tendency to have too many middle management and staff personnel are documented in Part I of this book, especially in Chapter 3. However, this "habit" has a serious human resource development dimension as well. The following are reasons for this:

- There is a tendency to lock up much of the company's human resources asset in middle management jobs.
- These middle management jobs have a strong tendency to use up the time of the line managers and each other in various control-related activities.

As a result, a company not only experiences the problems outlined in Chapter 3, but also fails to develop some of its best human resources to better carry out those market-related activities that the company needs to do to remain competitive. The company not only becomes inward looking and clumsy, but it trains its younger managers in this behavior.

It is also important to recognize that the real cost of staff and to a lesser extent middle managers is that they take up the time of others in the organization who must react to their initiatives. Also, like the rest of overhead, these jobs and their associated costs tend to grow faster than sales.

To contribute as a successful core policy, this suggested policy must consciously limit the company's focus on the kinds of activities associated with these jobs by limiting the number of jobs. If this can be done successfully, the company can benefit enormously by minimizing the problems described in Chapter 3 and, simultaneously, focusing the development of its managers on learning *to do better* those activities that contribute more directly to the company's competitive well-being.

Do Not "Hard Wire" Compensation to Any Analogued Goals, Even Total Company Profits

Nothing is harder on the human resource development process or the orderly deployment of company's resources than a compensation system "hard wired" to an analogued result. This is true even if the analogue is total company profits.

Even overall company profits in time frames such as one year, which are typically used in incentive-compensation programs, are highly unreliable as measures of success. They are also subject to numerous "legal" actions which can be used to manipulate them. A simple way to avoid these problems and protest the company's human and other off-balance-sheet assets is to have a policy that forbids "hard wiring" any incentive-compensation system.

If an incentive system is desired, it should be based on judgment in it that allows the people administering the plan to take into account all those things that the analogues cannot "see" or otherwise represent properly.

Although it only prevents a mistake, a policy that successfully prevents an incentive-compensation system that is "hard wired" to an analogue would certainly qualify as a core policy, since it would materially enhance the chances that the company would not fail to compensate its managers and thereby discourage them from deploying its assets, especially off-balance-sheet assets, in the company's best interest.

CONCLUSION

The real job of top management is to lead the company through the development and enforcement of insightful policies. This is the most effective way in which senior management can directly affect what is actually *done* within the company.

However, how to do this in the area of managing the company's human organization seems to be a lost art these days. Hopefully this chapter will shed some light on this very old problem.

CHAPTER 12

THOUGHTS ON IMPLEMENTATION

As suggested in Chapter 10, *it is much easier to conceptualize than it is to implement.* This is so true in business that implementation can be thought of as a separate discipline. That is, a bundle of management know-how that is separate from that which is being implemented and that can be used over and over as a business tries to implement different changes. For example, the problems faced in implementing a change in a company's credit policy and those it faces in successfully changing a product offering have more in common than many people realize.

This final chapter is intended to be helpful to readers in implementing changes in their organizations. Specifically, five topics will be discussed. While they will be discussed in the context of implementing changes relating to the issues covered in this book, there is also some value to be gained in terms of better understanding the overall problem of implementing change in the management process. The five topics are:

- The problems faced by those who are trying to escape the analogue management trap.
- The limitations of the control management style as a way to achieve change.
- The role of personal leadership.
- Policy as the vehicle through which senior management influences the corporation.
- The role of the chewable bite.

PROBLEMS FACED WHEN LEAVING THE ANALOGUE MANAGEMENT TRAP

The problems in the current American management process are found in its *assumptions,* not their execution. The current process looks like a seamless web with no apparent entry point for those who wish to change it in any fundamental way. As was pointed out in Chapter 1:

- The current generation of American managers have "grown up" using the present management technology. It is the only system they know. Furthermore, they succeeded in their organizations because they excelled at using the system.
- The American business intellectual community (business schools, business press, etc.) nas focused exclusively on the language and concepts of our present system. Efforts in other directions often seem like nonmanagement to managers themselves and to those who observe their performance.
- Much of American business is publicly held. The "public" ownership also has grown up understanding and believing the current management technology. They may not like some current results, but it is not clear (particularly to the managements of publicly held companies) that these outside owners are capable of understanding or willing to understand significant shifts in management behavior.

It can be argued that:

- No one wants to change the system.
- Even if managers wanted to change the system, they would not know where to start.
- Plenty of people will attempt to stop them if they try.

Therefore, changing the American management system should be extremely difficult. History seems to support this view. For most of a decade we have been unhappy with our results, yet precious little progress has been made in changing our management behavior in any fundamental way.

However, once one understands and comes to grips with the "analogue management trap," a change in the process does not have to be all *that* difficult as long as one does not begin to doubt the following fundamental conclusions:

- Analogues can *never* be the complete representations we would like them to be.
- Even if they were, we *cannot* manage the business *activities* by controlling to analogue results.
- Analogues are self-fulfilling, therefore, they are not reliable indicators of *real* accomplishment.

Further, as we have pointed out:

- There is no need to stop (and therefore have to explain why) using the analogues, particularly the financial system that companies normally use.
- "Tight" financial management actually *hurts* financial performance as reported by the financial system.
- Good management *is* picked up by the financial system.
- There are multiple options for changing the system that can be implemented by managers who are successful in the current system.

It is also *not* true that investors and lenders are not interested in longer term performance:

- The market is dominated by institutional investors, who have no choice but to invest.
- There are scores of companies with little or no earnings and many with earnings but no dividends that have had good stock prices for many successive years.
- Many lenders have large positions in companies that can only be liquidated if the companies prosper over several years.

In my view, a major reason Wall Street appears to be so short-run oriented is that management gives them little credable reason to be otherwise.

While there are very good reasons why companies will have difficulties in changing their management system, there is *absolutely* no reason why management teams with courage and conviction cannot escape the analogue trap and be rewarded for doing so. However, there are good reasons why this will be different and management should not be surprised when it is.

CONTROL MANAGEMENT IS A LIMITED STYLE FOR MAKING CHANGES

Analogue management almost always is accompanied by a management style I call "control management." Control management is characterized by negotiations between supervisors and subordinates in which the subordinate "commits" to attaining certain goals. The most obvious example of this is the way the financial plan is developed in most companies. However, it can be used in almost any circumstance—for example, to attain an MBO objective or even sell a particular customer.

The problem with control management is that *delegation* turns into *abdication*. The superior turns over all responsibility for actually accomplishing the commitment to the subordinate. The only obligation of the superior in this system is to successfully negotiate a goal with which he is satisfied and to hold the subordinate to it. In effect, *the need to actually perform has been handed to a supposedly less capable subordinate*. Further, there is no natural limit on this process. In theory, every corporate goal could wind up in the hands of first-level managers, who could then delegate to their employees.

In fact, in situations where the tasks to be accomplished are well within the knowledge and capability of the person to whom the task is being abdicated, this approach might work. Since this is really to form an *effort* management, and, presumably all that is needed to accomplish the goal is effort. However, in the real world of management things are not that simple. In this more complicated real world it is necessary for delegators to retain responsibility for their own performance and view the subordinates to whom they are delegating as helping them do their jobs.

Accomplishing change in particular has this characteristic, *since change is really trading one set of problems for another*. When the change is proposed, the current problems, which are being "traded away" from, can be better understood because they are familiar to management. The problems being "traded for" (the new problems) must be *imagined* and therefore cannot be understood as well.

As the change begins to be implemented, learning will, of necessity, occur as the new problems associated with it are better understood. The result is that often the change itself needs to be modified in light of the new knowledge. Abdication cuts off the abdicators from this learning process and often results in the subordinates, who have a much narrower understanding of the change and much less organizational authority, doing just what they are told and producing surprisingly bad results.

To accomplish anything there must be knowledge and motivation. We have seen how "control management" can cut the superior off from knowledge and therefore from effective control of the change process. Control management also tends to diminish motivation.

Often the subordinates come to understand that the change without modifications will be disappointing or even produce results much different than those that are intended. If they feel their superior does not want to hear bad news, that solving the problem without the superior's help is a performance measurement, they can feel trapped by their commitment. They must somehow deliver on it no matter what is learned. This approach motivates people to act in their own interest rather than work enthusiastically in the company's interest.

THE ROLE OF PERSONAL LEADERSHIP

The real role of management is to manage the company's resources in a way that creates value. This can *only be accomplished,* as we saw in Chapter 10, *through managing other people in the company's organization.* The question is, what the most effective way to do this is, particularly if one is attempting to accomplish a change. As we have seen, a process based on controlling people to commitments is not very effective although it may be the most popular style used by American managers today.

An approach based on personal leadership is much more effective. There has been much written about leadership and almost everyone seems to be in favor of it. One would think then that we would have plenty of business leaders and there would be little reason to continue to talk or write about it. In fact as we all know, effective business leaders are *not* plentiful. Analogue management, by promoting control management, is a major reason businesses are lacking in this area.

A simple definition of a leader is a person who has followers (as opposed to people under his control). The leader acquires these followers when he or she is *worth* following. In almost all cases this is because, among other things, the leader does not attempt to delegate risk to his subordinates while retaining the credit for their accomplishments. (Some would even say he keeps the risk and sheds the credit.)

This behavior tends to motivate subordinates to want to do what the leader wants to do, allowing him to have much better managerial control and also more knowledge since subordinates are not reluctant to give him "bad news." Making a change in a business is a high-risk situation where on-line knowledge and motivation are important. Therefore, leadership management works much better than control management as a way to accomplish it.

POLICY IS THE WAY TOP MANAGEMENT INFLUENCES THE CORPORATION

But *how* does a leadership-oriented management accomplish change other than through analogued targets? The answer is simple; it makes and enforces policies.

The effect of a policy is to cause the organization to do something that the senior management believes will cause the company to function better competitively in the longer run. The types of potential "core policies" discussed in Chapter 11 are examples of what some of these policies could be as senior management attempts to create the conditions that will produce a more competitive human organization. In addition, senior management makes (or fails to make) policies in the other areas of the business as well, for example product policy, distribution policy, pricing policy, and so forth. These policy decisions can have an enormous impact on a company's competitive position over a few short years.

Consider the decisions of the Ford Motor Company in the early 1980s under Phil Caldwell and the decisions of General Motors as both tried to respond to the Japanese challenge. Ford decided to focus on creating the best car in its class (the Taurus/Sable) and focus on manufacturing quality using improved but conventional manufacturing techniques. General Motors embarked on a huge automation program in its manufacturing plants to improve its quality and costs. Ford not only improved its market share at General Motors' expense, but also was able to surpass General Motors in product quality as well. Interestingly the financial analogue was able to pick this up. Ford's profits rose rapidly during the 1980s and in 1987 surpassed General Motors, although Ford still remained significantly smaller than General Motors.

However, it is usually impossible to *predict* with any *certainty or precision* the effect of policies on the analogued results of a company (particularly *in specific* time periods). This was certainly true at Ford when the aforementioned decisions were made. *Management must do what it believes is right and the consequences, analogued and otherwise, will be what they will be and occur when they do.*

This inability to predict can cause analogue managers to not concentrate on formulating the kinds of policies that will make their company a superior competitor over time. Instead they concentrate on things such as corporate planning exercises, which start with analogable outcomes, and make policies to support them. *This is logically impossible.* Managers must manage *activities,* not *outcomes.*

However, when senior management does not conscientiously strive to do the policy-making, it is done at other levels. The lower level executives simply do what they believe is in the company's best interest (or perhaps even their own). The effect of this is to diminish senior management influence over the company.

Alfred Sloan, the long-time (1918–1946) CEO of General Motors, is quoted as saying, "In the long run companies compete with policy." I would recommend Mr. Sloan's book *My Years with General Motors* as a practical example of how a senior manager and his team exerted enormous influences over what was then the country's largest industrial corporation. They accomplished this by consciously thinking of the challenges and opportunities faced by the company in the general economy and from its competitors and developing *policies* to be used to shape its response. They had, what might have been at the time the country's most sophisticated financial system. While they used this financial system, the reader will see that it was in no way central to their policy-making or to the implementation of their policies. They seemed to have understood its limitations and did not exceed them.

The most insidious characteristics of *control-oriented* analogue management is the way it can cut senior management off from truly influencing the company. While giving the impression that it gives management an almost hard-wired control of day-to-day operations, it actually separates it from true strategic management activities. The very device—policy—that senior management needs to use to shape and control the company's competitive stance is *incapable of fitting into the analogue management process.*

THE ROLE OF THE CHEWABLE BITE

Making a change is, in reality, an investment cycle. Most of the investment is human time and effort. Since the effort to make change occurs simultaneously with all the other activities of a business, it is usually a diversion of managers' time. Further, as we have seen, trying to make a change is a *learning* activity as the idea is converted into the reality.

Both the quality of the time and effort invested and the quality of the reaction to the learning experiences are enhanced by making changes in smaller increments than the ones normally chosen. Such increments can be called "chewable bites" (as in not getting one's mouth too full).

The following are real risks in making a change that is otherwise well-conceived:

- The people making the change run out of physical and emotional energy because they have to continue to "put out" but never seem to get anything back for their efforts.
- So much is learned about the negative aspects of the change that it appears to be a bad idea.

Both of these problems are ameliorated by dividing the project into a series of smaller projects. Doing so results in:

- Shortening of the payback cycle.
- Reducing what is learned to more manageable propositions.

Many managers are afraid to do this because they believe the "enemies" of the project will have opportunities to stop the overall change or modify it more to their (the "enemies") liking. Others believe that to behave this way is to demonstrate a lack of personal and organizational courage—the "big moves" for "big gains" theory.

In my experience these concerns are far outweighed by the benefits of starting a project knowing we are going to learn something we will want to adjust to and recognizing that nothing sells a project as being a good idea better than having a little success.

Using chewable bites is particularly effective in organizations that have a history of trying to force change down the throats of people who, they believe "naturally" resist change.

The change makers soon learn that much of this "natural" resistance is for good reasons and can therefore separate the reasoned resistance from emotional or personal objections. Once the separation occurs it is amazing how few "natural" resisters are left and how little support they can generate for their ideas.

CONCLUSION

The seeds of our analogue management process were well sprouted when I first entered the business world in 1957. Business management was caught up along with the other social sciences in the quantification craze of that time that was itself probably a reaction to the success of the physical sciences.

I remember a period when:

- Operations research was going to revolutionize the management process using techniques such as linear programming and "gaming theory."
- Personality and aptitude tests were going to help us choose presidents and promote business executives.
- Psychologists and sociologists were attempting to make their experiments more meaningful by making them more quantitative.
- Econometrics was just starting to be used.

Is it any wonder then, that given this atmosphere and the extraordinary advantage American business enjoyed following World War II, American management fell into the analogue management trap? Furthermore, the major industrial competitors in Europe and Japan seem to believe in quantification as well. Didn't they crowd our business schools and visit our companies trying to learn about our management system?

We have subsequently become more insightful about the limits of quantification in the social sciences. Economies are proving to be very difficult to predict using mathematical models as is human behavior. Operations research techniques, in spite of our having far more powerful computers than we did in the 1950s, play a relatively small role in the management decision-making process.

It is now time to take the final steps and put the accounting system and other business analogues back into their proper places in the business management process. No matter how much more we tinker with the accounting system, it will still retain its basic limitation of needing financial transactions. The other analogues can tell us bits and pieces of information but can never give a complete picture of a decision let alone an answer.

I would like to tell my grandchildren, when they are older and join what, I hope and believe, will be much more competitive American companies, that I was around when American management turned the corner.

INDEX

A

Abdication, and delegation, 187
Abernathy, William J., 4, 5
Accounting system, 13
  and expectations, 21–25
  and financial transactions, 22–23
  as flawed analogue, 20–32, 194
  and international management
      process, 30–32
  and short-run behavior, 24
  small-business dilemma, 26–29
  and time period problem, 25–26
Across-the-board cuts, 127–28
Activity, business, 121
Administration, and expense, 108
Advantage
  continuous competitive, 149–66
  and strategy, 149–53
AICPA, 15
Allocation, and incremental costs, 117
American corporations
  and analogue management, 33–49
  and nimbleness, 39–42
Analogue
  accounting system as, 20–32, 194
  finance as, 31–32
  insightful use of, 85–94
  macro- and micro-, 89
  management. See Analogue
      management
  and reality, 7–13
  and technical flaws, 61–77
Analogue management
  and accounting system flaws, 20–32,
      194
  and American corporations, 33–49
  background, 3–7

Analogue management—(continued)
  and control, 48
  and cooperation, 38–39
  defined, 7
  fundamental errors, 10–11
  and implementation, 184–94
  and incentive-compensation systems,
      44–46
  issues to understand, 18–19
  and managers, 46–49
  and problems in leaving, 185–87
  and self-fulfillment, 14–16
  and short-run activities, 33–36
  and top management, 33–36
  trap, 7–11, 16–19, 31–32
  and value-creation process, 36–38
Analysis, strategic. See Strategic analysis
Assets, 23, 37–38, 161
Attitude, and management, 46–49

B

Balance sheet, and value-creation
      process, 36–38
Bank of America, 12, 58
Behavior, irrational, 58–60
Bites, chewable, 191–93
Brandt, Steven C., 33
Budget
  and actual, 116–17
  flexible, 104, 121
  and overhead suppliers, 125–26
  reports, department, 70–74
  and programmed expenses, 135
Business, core. See Core business
Business activity, 121
Business units, 38

C

Caldwell, Phil, 190
Capital investment, 89
Cash cow, 156, 157, 158
Cash flow, 51, 58
Caterpillar Corp., 143
CBS. *See* Columbia Broadcasting
System (CBS)
Chewable bites, role of, 191–93
Clauson, Thomas, 12
Columbia Broadcasting System (CBS),
58, 59
Compensation, unhooking, 180–83
Competition, and surplus, 149
Competitive advantage, continuous. *See*
Advantage
"Competitive Advantage to Corporate
Strategy, From," 58
Competitiveness, American, 6, 7
Competitive Strategy, 58, 150, 154
Competitor, and service, 143
Continental Illinois, 58
Continuous competitive advantage,
149–66
concept of, 164–66
Control
cost, 99–109, 107, 108
and control management, 187–88
and factory costs, 100–107
and management, 48, 98–99
and management-control systems,
96–97
and measurement, 75–76, 109,
117–18
and overhead, 121–23
and selling and administrative
expense, 108
Control Data Corporation, 22
Control management. *See* Control
Cooperation
and analogue management, 38–39
and organizations, 177–78
Core business, role of, 149,154–58
Core competitive policy, and horizontal
management, 167–83

Core policies, 168–72, 175–83,
189–91
Corporate plan, 14
Corporate strategy, 154
Corporations
American, 33–49
and cooperation, 38–39
and growth, 50–60
and improvement, 54
inward-looking, 42–44
and objectives, 56, 161–62
and planning, 56–57
and strategic analysis, 55, 57–58
Cost
direct and indirect, 106
factory, 100–107
incremental, 117
and overhead, 119–36
product, 63–70, 109–17
and programmed expenses, 135
and service, 146
Cost control, 107, 108
and manufacturing, 99–109
and service industries, 108
Counterproductivity, 44–46
Cray, Seymour, 22
Cray Research, 22
Customer, and service, 143
Cuts, across-the-board, 127–28

D

Data, classification of, 95–96
Datamation, 51
Delegation, and abdication, 187
Delivery system, and service, 142–46
Department budget reports, erroneous,
70–74
Departments, direct and indirect, 65,
66, 110, 111, 114
Development
and management, 46–49
and organizations, 163–64
Differentiation, and products, 137
Digital Equipment Corporation, 41

Direct costs, 106
Direct departments, 65, 66, 110, 111, 114
Distribution system, 23
Dog, 51, 58
Domino's Pizza, 143

E

Expectations, and accounting system, 21–25
Expense
and administration, 108
programmed, 135

F

FASB. *See* Financial Accounting Standards Board (FASB)
Federal Express, 143
Finance
as analogue, 31–32
and management, 91–94, 136
performance, 90–91
transactions, and accounting, 22–23
Financial Accounting Standards Board (FASB), 13, 15, 30, 61, 66
Fixed costs, 67, 69
Flexible budgeting, 104, 121
Focus, and strategy, 151–52
Ford Motor Company, 173, 190
Formal corporate planning, 55
Fortune, 50, 51
Full-absorption product cost system, 66, 68, 69

G

GAAP. *See* Generally Accepted Accounting Principles (GAAP)
Gap, planning, 56
Geneen, Harold, 34
Generally Accepted Accounting Principles (GAAP), 13, 23, 99, 115

General Motors Corporation, 190, 191
Goals, and compensation, 182–83
Growth, 85
causes of, 53–54
and improvement, 52
and management, 54–60
and overhead, 124–27
and success, 50–60

H

Hart, Christopher, W. L., 143
Harvard Business Review (HBR), 4, 5–6, 143
Hayes, Robert H., 4, 5
HBR. *See Harvard Business Review* (HBR)
Horizontal management, 172–75
and core competitive policies, 167–83
and manager transfers, 178–80
Human resources, and management, 177–78

I

IBM. *See* International Business Machines (IBM)
Implementation, 184–94
and personal leadership, 188–89
Improvement
and corporations, 54
and growth, 52
INC., 51
Incentive-compensation systems, 44–46
Incremental costs, and allocation, 117
Indirect costs, 106
Indirect departments, 65, 66, 110, 111, 114
Industries, service, 108
Internal Revenue Service (IRS), 66, 99, 115
International Business Machines (IBM), 161
International management process, and accounting, 30–32

Inventory, 23
Investment, capital, 89
Inward-looking corporations, 42–44
IRS. *See* Internal Revenue Service (IRS)
ITT, 34

J

Japan
   and core policy, 170, 171
   and current American reactions, 4–5
   and fixed costs, 69
   and JIT, 5
   and organizational development, 163
   and quality, 43
JIT. *See* Just-in-time material
   management (JIT)
Just-in-time material management (JIT),
   5, 175

L

"Large American Corporations and
   Communist Societies Are Centrally
   Planned," 41
Lawrence, Paul R., 180
Leadership, personal, 188–89
Life cycles, and products, 27
Line-management, 162–63
Long-range Plan, 14
Lorsch, Jay W., 180

M

Macroanalogue, 89
Management
   analogue. *See* Analogue management
   and control, 98–99
   and control management, 187–88
   current problems, 4
   and finance, 91–94, 136
   and growth, 54–60
   horizontal, 167, 172–75
   and human resources, 177–78
   and implementation, 184–94
   international, 30–32

Management—(*continued*)
   and irrational behavior, 58–60
   JIT. *See* Just-in-time material
     management (JIT)
   line-, 162–63
   and maturity, 47
   middle, 181–82
   and organizations, 189–91
   and overhead, 119–36, 129–36
   and performance, development, and
     attitude, 46–49
   and personal leadership, 188–89
   and policy, 189–91
   and problems in changing, 185–87
   and reality, 11–13
   reports, 95–118
   and self-fulfillment, 14–16
   and service, 137–48
   and service wrapper, 139–41
   top, 33–36, 49
   and transfers, 178–80
   and universal truths, 175–76
Management-control systems, 96–97
"Managing Our Way to Economic
   Decline," 4, 5
Manpower Incorporated, 143
Manufacturing
   and cost control, 99–109
   and product costing flaws, 63–70
   and product cost measurement, 109–17
Market position, 23
Masters of Business Administration
   (MBA), 3
Maturity, and management, 47
MBA. *See* Masters of Business
   Administration (MBA)
Measurement
   and control, 75–76, 109, 117–18
   limits of, 116
   and performance, 110
   and product cost in manufacturing,
     109–17
   systems, 98
Microanalogue, 89
Morgan Stanley, 119
My Years with General Motors, 191

N

Nimbleness, and American
corporations, 39–42

O

Objectives, and corporations, 56,
161–62
Olsen, Ken, 41
Organization and Environment, 180
Organizations
building elements, 161–64
and cooperation, 177–78
and development, 163–64
and management, 189–91
role of, 149, 158–64
Output
and overhead, 131–32
and producers, 132–33
Overhead
and control, 121–23
defined, 120–21
and growth, 124–27
and management, 119–36, 129–36
and outputs produced, 131–33
and products, 122
and spending, 130–32
suppliers, 125–26
Overhead-management system, 133–36

P

Performance
and finance, 90–91
and management, 46–49
and measurement, 110
Personal leadership, role of, 188–89
Planning, and corporations, 56–57
Planning gap, 56
Policy
core, 168–72, 175–83, 189–91
core competitive, 167–83
and Japan, 170, 171
and management, 189–91

Porter, Michael, 58, 59, 150, 152,154
"Power of Unconditional Guarantees,
The," 143
Product
costing, erroneous, 63–70
cost measurement, 109–17
and differentiation, 137
and life cycles, 27
portfolio, 23
quality, 23
and overhead, 122
Production, and overhead, 131–33
Productivity, counter-. *See*
Counterproductivity
Profit
centers, 38
and compensation, 182–83
and growth, 52
Programmed expenses, 135

Q

Quality, 23

R

Raiders, 59
Reality, and analogue, 7–13
Reports
budget, 70–74
management, 95–118
Reputation, 23

S

Sales, and growth, 52
SEC. *See* Securities and Exchange
Commission (SEC)
Securities Acts, 15
Securities and Exchange Commission
(SEC), 12, 15, 54, 61, 86
Self-fulfillment, and management,
14–16
Selling, and control and administrative
expense, 108

Service
    and competitor, 143
    and cost, 146
    and customer, 143
    delivery system, 142–46
    difficulty of, 138–39
    industries, and cost control, 108
    and management, 137–48
    and wrappers, 137, 139–44,
        146–48
Short-run activities, and analogue
    management, 33–36
Short-run behavior
    and accounting, 24
    and growth, 53
Sloan, Alfred, 191
Small-business dilemma, 26–29
Spending, and overhead, 130–32
Staff jobs, 181–82
Star, 51, 58
Strategic analysis, 55, 57–58
    and corporations, 57–58
*Strategic Planning in Emerging
    Companies*, 33
Strategy
    and competitive advantage, 149–53
    and core business, 149, 154–58
    corporate, 154
    and focus, 151–52
    formal, 149
    and organization, 149, 158–64
    and service wrapper, 146–48
Success, and growth, 50–60

Suppliers, overhead, 125–26
Surplus, and competition, 149

T

Technical flaws, and analogues, 61–77
Third World countries, 59
Time period problem, and accounting,
    25–26
Top-down orientation, 33
Top management. *See* Management
Turnaround, 20, 21

U

Units, 38
Universal truths, and management,
    175–76

V

Value-creation process, and balance
    sheet, 36–38

W

Wall Street, 16
World War II, and American
    management evaluation, 3–4, 193
Wrappers, and service, 137, 139–44,
    146–48
Write-off, 21